HOW TO OPEN & OPERATE
A FINANCIALLY SUCCESSFUL

CHILD CARE
SERVICE

WITH COMPANION CD-ROM

BY TINA MUSIAL

HOW TO OPEN & OPERATE A FINANCIALLY SUCCESSFUL CHILD CARE SERVICE — WITH COMPANION CD-ROM

Copyright © 2007 by Atlantic Publishing Group, Inc.
1405 SW 6th Ave. • Ocala, Florida 34471 • 800-814-1132 • 352-622-1875–Fax
Web site: www.atlantic-pub.com • E-mail: sales@atlantic-pub.com
SAN Number: 268-1250

ISBN-13: 978-1-60138-115-6   ISBN-10: 1-60138-115-8

Library of Congress Cataloging-in-Publication Data

Musial, Tina, 1973-
  How to open & operate a financially successful child care service, with companion CD-Rom / by Tina Musial.
     p. cm.
  Includes bibliographical references and index.
  ISBN-13: 978-1-60138-115-6 (alk. paper)
  ISBN-10: 1-60138-115-8 (alk. paper)
  1. Child care services--United States--Handbooks, manuals, etc. 2. Day care centers--United States--Handbooks, manuals, etc. 3. New business enterprises--United States--Handbooks, manuals, etc. I. Title. II. Title: How to open and operate a financially successful child care service.

  HQ778.63.M87 2007
  362.71'2068--dc22
                            2007025038

EDITOR: Tracie Kendziora • tkendziora@atlantic-pub.com
INTERIOR DESIGN: Vickie Taylor • vtaylor@atlantic-pub.com

Printed in the United States

Printed on Recycled Paper

We recently lost our beloved pet "Bear," who was not only
our best and dearest friend but also the "Vice President of
Sunshine" here at Atlantic Publishing. He did not receive
a salary but worked tirelessly 24 hours a day to please his
parents. Bear was a rescue dog that turned around and
showered myself, my wife Sherri, his grandparents Jean, Bob
and Nancy and every person and animal he met (maybe not
rabbits) with friendship and love. He made a lot of people
smile every day.

We wanted you to know that a portion of the profits of this
book will be donated to The Humane Society of
the United States.

–Douglas & Sherri Brown

THE HUMANE SOCIETY
OF THE UNITED STATES ©

The human-animal bond is as old as human history. We cherish our animal companions for their unconditional affection and acceptance. We feel a thrill when we glimpse wild creatures in their natural habitat or in our own backyard.

Unfortunately, the human-animal bond has at times been weakened. Humans have exploited some animal species to the point of extinction.

The Humane Society of the United States makes a difference in the lives of animals here at home and worldwide. The HSUS is dedicated to creating a world where our relationship with animals is guided by compassion. We seek a truly humane society in which animals are respected for their intrinsic value, and where the human-animal bond is strong.

Want to help animals? We have plenty of suggestions. Adopt a pet from a local shelter, join The Humane Society and be a part of our work to help companion animals and wildlife. You will be funding our educational, legislative, investigative and outreach projects in the U.S. and across the globe.

Or perhaps you'd like to make a memorial donation in honor of a pet, friend or relative? You can through our Kindred Spirits program. And if you'd like to contribute in a more structured way, our Planned Giving Office has suggestions about estate planning, annuities, and even gifts of stock that avoid capital gains taxes.

Maybe you have land that you would like to preserve as a lasting habitat for wildlife. Our Wildlife Land Trust can help you. Perhaps the land you want to share is a backyard—that's enough. Our Urban Wildlife Sanctuary Program will show you how to create a habitat for your wild neighbors.

So you see, it's easy to help animals. And The HSUS is here to help.

The Humane Society of the United States
2100 L Street NW
Washington, DC 20037
202-452-1100
www.hsus.org

AUTHOR DEDICATION

To Mom and Dad for all of the nurturing, and to Mitchell and Sean for allowing me to pass it on...

CONTENTS

Chapter 5: Federal & State Requirements 69

Chapter 6: Business Needs 75

Chapter 7: Promoting Your Business 93

CHAPTER 8: GOALS & OBJECTIVES 121

PART 3: OPEN FOR BUSINESS 125

CHAPTER 9: BUSINESS POLICIES 127

CHAPTER 10: BUSINESS PRACTICES 143

CHAPTER 11: ACCREDITATION & EDUCATION ... 161

CHAPTER 12: CHILDREN'S POLICIES 169

FOREWORD

By Kathy Feigly

Tina Musial, in *How to Open & Operate a Financially Successful Child Care Service*, provides an introductory perspective for the budding entrepreneur in the business of child care. The text flows smoothly from one topic to the next as she poses reflective comments on the pros and cons of each dimension of getting started. During the conceptual phase Tina analyzes the different types of programs, locations, and facilities. As the dream of ownership becomes a reality, she guides you toward developing your business plan and meeting your financial goals. In the final stage, she reviews important policies, procedures, and reporting requirements.

Marketing opportunities, administrative considerations, and record keeping overviews are all presented. She elaborates on forming the team necessary to steer a new business down the road to success. Samples of forms and policies are provided to give professionals a jump start, complete with resource lists, contacts, and curriculum suggestions.

In child care you are dealing with a parent's most valuable possession and, therefore, you must be very thorough in covering all the regulatory aspects and issues surrounding conducting a safe, successful, and developmentally appropriate environment for children to grow.

How to Open & Operate a Successful Child Care Service touches on many of these aspects, as Tina leads you on a journey from conceptualization to realization of a dream and becoming an entrepreneur in the world of child care.

As the founder of Kangaroo Kids Child Care & Learning Center and an experienced child care provider, I found the information contained in this book extremely helpful. For those who want to start a child care business, this book will teach you everything you need to know. Even practiced providers, such as myself, stand to glean some information from this well-written, informative book. Tina has done an excellent job writing a guide for anyone interested in child care services.

Kathy Feigley is the founder of Kangaroo Kids Child Care and Learning Center, which is one of only 7 percent of schools nationwide to earn accreditation by the National Association for the Education of Young Children. She is currently the host of the cable television show, Today's Child, *reaching over 300,000 families. Her past experiences include appearing as a guest on the Regis Philbin cable show and Channel 5 news.*

Kathy earned her degree from College of New Jersey, is Vice President of the Early Childhood Directors Association, serves on the advisory board for Raritan Valley Community College, and is Public Relations Chairman for the

Branchburg Rotary. For over 30 years she has successfully trained and mentored teachers, coaches, and children in various educational programs.

As publicity chairman for the Branchburg Rotary she has earned Public Relations Awards; her press releases have appeared in Courier News, Branchburg News, and the Somerset Reporter. She is also a contributing author to Physical Education and Sport for the Secondary School Student.

Kathy was named Outstanding Business Person of the Year for Somerset County, has been the recipient of the Somerset County Economic Vitality Award, and the recipient of Governor Whitman's Bright Beginnings Grant. She has received a Certificate of Special Congressional Recognition.

Kathleen Feigley
Kangaroo Kids Child Care and Learning Center
1047 Route 28
Branchburg, NJ 08876
Phone: 908-231-7800
Fax: 908-231-9847
E-mail: kangarookidsabc@aol.com
Web site: **http://kangarookidschildcare.com**
Host of Today's Child

Accredited by NAEYC's
National Academy
of Early Childhood
Programs

INTRODUCTION

You are looking for a way to earn some money. You may have young children at home, but you do not relish the idea of taking them to child care every day while you work. In addition, with the expense of child care for two, three, or more children, you may owe more in one day than what you even make. On the other hand, you may like children and want to be with children, but do not have a teaching certificate or the time to get one. There is a simple and rewarding way you can be with children and earn a fabulous income: open your own child care center.

A child care center can be a rewarding experience mentally and financially. A small, home center can keep you home with your children, but still earn money in the process. Buying an established child care center will take a lot of capital, but you will also see profits more quickly. Opening a new center with more children can earn you more money since it has new features, new equipment, and young families, but it will also have a bigger price tag and more start up responsibilities.

No matter which type of center you want, or believe is best for you and your situation, this book is intended to give you a complete understanding of the policies and practices you will need to implement to start and run your own child care center. There are resources for specific state information, forms to use, and tips on policy making. The only thing left to do is figure out what type of child care center will work best for you. So let us get started. Get out your pencil, make some notes, and have fun reading about how you can open and operate your very own successful child care center.

"You can learn many things from children.

How much patience you have, for instance."

~ Franklin P. Jones

Part 1

I Want to Open a Child Care Center, but Where Do I Start?

Before you can open a business, you need to decide what kind of business you want to run. When caring for children there are several ways to go about doing business. There are different levels of child care centers you can successfully open and operate: You can purchase an existing center, start a completely new center, or operate out of your home.

Each child care center operation has unique features that might work for your financial abilities, family needs, and economical situation. Conversely, each type has features that definitely might not work for your personality or financial situation. You will need to consider all of the pros and cons to each type of child care operation before making any decision or spending any money up front.

ABC

1

TYPES OF CHILD CARE CENTERS

There are different ways to go about running a child care center. First, you can open a home child care where you are licensed to care for a specific number of children in your home. Second, you can purchase an existing child care and restructure it to fit your needs — change services offered, hours, families served, etc. Last, you can open and operate a brand new child care center, with or without a franchise. All three are viable options.

There are also certain things to consider when deciding on which type of business fits your needs the best. Depending on how much capital you have to work with is the biggest determinate of which route you take. However, there are many other variables to consider, too. If you do not have money to invest in building a facility or purchasing an existing one, home child care may be the safest route to go. Start up costs are minimal, especially if you already have children who have toys and supplies for other children to use. If you do not have the start up money, but do not want to stay in your home either, you can find financial backing in the form of an investor or through business loans.

Before deciding on your business style, take into consideration your personality type. Are you comfortable managing and speaking to several people at one time? Can you handle the responsibility of scheduling and training staff members? Do you make a budget and stick to it easily? If you do not mind being the front person for PR, advertising, and leading a business, then a large center could work for you. If you are shy and do not like to manage others, a smaller center or home child care is probably a better choice.

There are many other small details to consider before opening a business: Is there a need for a large child care center in your town? The next town? What size childcare facility can your town support? Who is your competition? Do you have any competition?

Following are some pros and cons in regard to opening each type of center. Of course, each person will have their own preferences, and the decision is personal.

Existing Child Care Centers

An existing child care center may be large or medium sized. For whatever reason, the current owners are selling it, along with the building and its contents. The business may be independent or a franchise.

The Pros of Purchasing an Existing Child Care Center

Purchasing an existing child care center is a wise option if you have financial backing or investors to help you. An established business will cost a lot of money because you are also purchasing the clientele that accompanies it. Getting the clientele and the publicity started for a new business is hard work and time consuming, so having these things established is helpful.

Families in the area might already know about the center and its policies and practices, either firsthand, by word of mouth, or because they drive by it everyday. Since it has already been in the community, chances are some type of marketing and advertising campaign has already been established, and you will just need to expand on it a little.

The child care center will be stocked with toys, equipment, and food. There will be no need to shop for all of the supplies up front unless certain items need updating. Less shopping means fewer start up costs. The less money you spend on equipment can be more money towards programs or payroll in the future.

Another positive note with an existing center is that it will already have a full staff. The decision will be yours if you keep all of them or not. Look through their records and history to help you decide. If they are missing some training skills, like CPR or first aid, you can offer the classes. If they refuse, they can be terminated.

As with any existing business, the policies are already in place. You may need to revise them to fit your style, but a revision is easier and quicker than starting from scratch and reinventing the wheel.

You may have the benefit of a corporate franchise to back you up. Franchises may have a bigger budget, a system for substitute staff member swapping, and money for going over budget, covering unexpected expenses, and fixing problems that may appear in daily operations.

A franchise will also connect you, as the owner, with other people to whom you can relate. Each owner is in the exact same boat, and you have similar problems, situations, and experiences to share. This group may also offer support and encouragement when you need it most.

The Cons of Purchasing an Existing Child Care Center

Negative publicity. If the owners are selling because they have been forced out due to bad business practices or decisions, you may have some PR work to do. Even with advertising new ownership, you may have some trust issues to overcome. The expense of spinning positive marketing and advertising new ownership may make it just as expensive as if you had started with a brand new center.

Also, you may not like the families that are being served by the child care center. If you have families who are delinquent in payment or do not agree with the new policies you plan to implement, you may have to decide if you will excuse them from your services. It will take a while for turnover to reflect your preferred style of families.

Since both layout and location are set in stone you cannot change either one. The layout or location of your building may not be ideal, but you are stuck – at least for a while.

The layout of your child care center may be a little funky and not great for efficiency, but it is what you have to work with. You could always remodel; however, remodeling will cost money and possible shut down time. Shut down time will also cost you money. If you are going to spend a lot of money to remodel, you might want to think about buying brand new and beginning from scratch for the same or close to the same price.

Home Child Care Centers

A home child care center licenses you to care for up to six children in your house. There is also an option to have a group child care center, in which you are allowed to watch 12 children in your home, but you must hire an assistant.

The Pros of Operating an In Home Child Care Center

You get to work out of your home, using toys and equipment you may already have. It is a win-win situation if you have small children, since you can still earn an income and stay home with your children.

A home child care center takes little capital up front. The only start up expenses will be the licensing fees, office supplies, and food. A home child care center is a smart choice when you have little capital to invest.

A home child care center offers the family only one contact person. There is one consistent provider for the child, so his or her routine and schedule do not change, nor does his or her caregiver. Large centers often run shifts of employees, giving the family several different contact people. This can also make for confusion or inconsistent discipline. The small group setting provides more personalized care and the chance for more in-depth one on one time.

Working out of the home gives you the opportunity to write off home expenses on your income taxes. The depreciation of any household items, the cost of electricity, water, garbage, Internet, cable, and supplies can all be written off at tax time, and might add up more money in your bank account.

The Cons of Operating an In Home Child Care Center

You do get to work at home and be with your children, but you also cannot get away. You will have little chance to get out of the house during the day unless you have a vehicle large enough to safely carry everyone. Because you are taking care of other children, your children may miss extra-curricular activities if you cannot readily transport everyone. And you are not able to leave, even if you have evening plans, if a parent arrives late to pick up a child.

The appearance of your house will represent your business. The grass will need to be mowed, the yard will need to be kept up, and the weeds should be pulled regularly. A prospective family may drive by before they call to get information. If they do not like what they see, they will not call. No matter how clean the inside of your house is or how great of a program you run, you may lose business based on the outside's appearance.

When working at home, your house will also get used. The carpet will have more wear, the toys will be used daily, cleaning will be required more often, and so on. The toll of daily use may not be what you want for your house and its appreciation value. You can write off certain aspects of your business, but the wear will still show. After several years, you may need to replace flooring or paint the walls.

Since you are always home, you will have little interaction with other adults. This is not to say you will be completely isolated; there are groups to join for other home child care providers, but you will have much less contact with "the outside" world on a daily basis.

The family pet may need to be locked away during the day. This is partially for the pet's benefit, as they might not enjoy added attention. If being surrounded by children on a daily basis does not suit them, you do not want to find out the hard way. Even the tiniest accident could lead to a lawsuit or charges filed. In addition, even in extreme situations, it could result in the loss of your beloved family pet.

Another worst-case scenario is if a child has an allergy to a pet. You will have to decide if shutting away a cat is remedy enough or if the case is more severe. If the allergic reaction is severe, you will need to decide between the pet and the child.

NEW CHILD CARE CENTER

A new child care center may be in the form of a franchise's expansion. You may have decided to take the plunge and go from an in home child care center to a large center that needs a full time staff. A new child care center could also be a brand new start up goal that you finally decided to pursue after several years in the business.

The Pros of Opening a Brand New Child Care Center

A new child care center is a great way to start fresh and be involved with every aspect of creating your business. You can draw the floor plans if you are building a center from scratch. You can be creative with the room designs, the layout of play areas, and even design a playground with all of the hottest and newest features. You can choose to be very simplistic and minimal to keep your expenses down, or you can be very creative and elaborate and design incredible play structures for the inside and outside. The only limiting factor is your budget.

You can have complete control over the programs, the staff, the training, and the equipment. You get to choose what you want, and you do not have to follow what a boss tells you to do. The freedom to choose can be exhilarating.

A child care center that is brand new can have state of the art equipment, handicap accessible rooms, and an awesome playground. If you can afford state of the art equipment, you may be able to provide for families who have disabilities. You may be opening yours doors to a wider audience that a traditional, older center cannot accommodate.

The families that begin with your center can be hand picked by you. You can go through an interview process with every family, and choose not to accept anyone. Make sure you are not discriminating, however, as that could land you in legal trouble.

You will get to hire all of the staff and train them to your standards. You can pick the best of the best and mold them as you see fit.

You can also implement any educational program in your new center. If you want to follow a teaching method, it is your prerogative. You will need to disclose any methods that you do choose to the family, as they have the ultimate choice in how and what they want their child to learn.

The Cons of Opening a Brand New Child Care Center

The downside of a new center is the cost. All of those state of the art features come with a high price tag. Building costs can be very high in some states and cities, too. The materials alone for a center would be expensive, and you need to add in the cost for the special equipment, buildings materials, contractors, etc.

There are many regulations that need to be followed, not only for code, but also for state licensing requirements. Special wiring, plumbing, fire alarm systems, security systems, and bathroom facilities may be required that cost above and beyond what a normal contractor will do. Additional fees or specialized contractors may be needed for the completion of your building project.

New equipment such as toys, art supplies, tables, chairs, kitchen supplies, and outdoor equipment can add up fast. Buying for a large center also requires a lot of inventory, and inventory takes up space and money.

To pay for all of your projected costs, you may need help. You may need to find additional financing from partners or silent investors to help you complete your project. A silent partner or financing company may take away some of your decision making capabilities. There will be extra preparation time for paperwork and getting financial approval before you can begin the necessary start up operations.

Another downside is starting from the bottom with advertising and publicity for families who will use your services. If you do not know how to advertise or market yourself and your business, you will need to find someone that does. Having adequate PR in the beginning of a business venture can set you in the right direction, for a fee. If you do it yourself to save money and do it wrong or not at all, you can make the road to profitability that much more difficult to achieve.

No matter what type of child care center you choose to open and operate, there will be state licensing forms to fill out. In order to claim all of the tax benefits and be legal, a license is necessary. The license for each type of center will vary slightly, as it states how many children can be under your care and the care of any staff members.

Three different in home child care providers all agreed that filling out the required paperwork for the state of Michigan was tedious. Michigan has one of the most thorough licensing procedures to go through; there are health forms to fill out, questionnaires, policies to read and sign, and paperwork to fill out for each child. You never know when an inspector may drop in, so you always want to have your paperwork done and up to date. Having your paperwork filled out ahead of time is worth the effort, one provider from Midland, Michigan adds.

When you are opening a franchise child care center, you will need to follow all the corporate rules. There may also be expensive corporate fees to maintain the corporate image and to be able to use the logo and identity. Certain permissions may be required for family interviews, paperwork, and the hiring of your staff by higher up corporate officers.

A franchise owner for a large child care chain on the East Coast had nothing but praise for her system. The corporate offices provided her with not only the papers to fill out, but also counseled her on how and when to do it. She had everything she needed, without having to call agency after agency or spend hours online searching for the right forms.

"Even when freshly washed and relieved of all obvious confections, children tend to be sticky."
~ Fran Lebowitz

A B C

2

REQUIREMENTS

Having pondered all the pros and cons, looked at the facts and figures, and maybe even talked to a few people in the child care business, you know your direction. Now it is time to get into the nitty gritty of seeing your dream become a reality.

Every state has a regulating committee that oversees childcare licensing, and you will need to be in contact with them. This agency will guide you through the process of becoming licensed and should be able to answer all of your questions or direct you to someone who can. Some states require more steps than others, but each state's guidelines need to be followed in order to acquire your license as quickly and effortlessly as possible.

Separate from each state are home child care centers located on military bases. Each branch of the military has their own set of regulations for those centers. They need to be licensed, file extensive paperwork, and meet safety regulations, just like any state would, but the military governs their license. One home child care provider who lived on a military based in North Carolina was surprised by the safety requirements needed. Every cupboard door in the house had to have a child lock on it.

The first step will be filling out the initial paperwork with your name, address, phone number, and social security number. You will need to submit your social security number and the social security numbers of any other adults living in your home for a background check, if it is a home child care center you wish to open. The background check reveals any charges filed in the past involving children. The background check is very thorough and usually completed by the FBI. If you are opening a larger center and will be hiring a staff, they will also be subjected to a background search.

In the initial paperwork, you will also need to state what type of center you intend to open. Each type of child care center will require a different set of inspections to be performed prior to opening.

INSPECTIONS

In Home Group and Day Care Centers

You will have an inspection by a state representative, who will inspect your house much like an appraiser or home inspector would. They look for potentially unsafe conditions with the plumbing, electrical, and HVAC systems. They also have a checklist to see if you meet specifications set up by your state.

SAMPLE CHECKLIST

- ❑ A clearly marked, lit exit sign
- ❑ An egress window that functions if the child care operation is in the basement
- ❑ A written fire escape plan
- ❑ A written tornado drill plan
- ❑ An appropriate napping area for each child
- ❑ A sample daily schedule

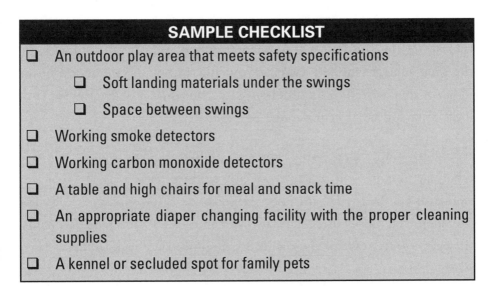

The checklist will vary between states and is usually several pages long. The inspector is looking for anything that could potentially be unsafe for children.

If you do not pass the inspection, the agency will provide you with a list of improvements you need to make. Some improvements can be in progress while you are opening, such as completing a tornado drill plan or setting up your outdoor play area. You are given 30, 60, or 90 days to fix any of the citations before another inspection take place to check to make sure they have been corrected. Other incidents may be major and have to be fixed before you are allowed to open, such as having no smoke detectors or inadequate bathroom facilities. The state will let you know the status of your licensing and how soon you have to fix any and all problems before they return.

Once you pass the initial inspection, you will also need to have a physical examination. The physical will be general in nature to check for any conditions that may limit your capacity to care for children. Additional testing in certain states is required for such diseases like tuberculosis or hepatitis. Any adult who will be living in your home or assisting with the care of the children will need to be tested. When the results are in, the state agency will add them to your file. Other specific blood borne illnesses are checked for in different states, but they vary greatly. See your local licensing agency for details.

A food program inspection, if you elect to join such a program, will also take place before you can open. Many states offer a program that sets standards for the food that can be served to the children in your care. For providers that follow these standards and enroll their children and menus, they get a percentage of the cost of food reimbursed back to them.

The food program inspector will initially come and check the equipment in your kitchen. He or she will make sure you have adequate preparation space and utensils to serve the children. A sample menu plan for a week or month ahead of time may need to be written out so he or she can approve it. Monthly paperwork is required, and must be sent in and approved before you receive your reimbursement check for the food.

Other requirements you may need as an individual may be CPR and first aid training. Michigan requires all providers and their assistants (employees) to have adult, child, and infant CPR certification yearly. A basic first aid class must also be taken by everyone that assists in your child care operation. The certification papers provided by the teacher must be copied and sent to the state to be kept on file.

LARGE CHILD CARE CENTERS

A large center will also require an inspection prior to licensing. The inspector, sent by the state, is looking for any condition that might prove detrimental to the child in a large setting.

CHECKLIST FOR A LARGE CENTER

- ❑ A written fire plan at each doorway
- ❑ A written tornado drill posted in each room
- ❑ A clearly marked, lit exit sign at each door
- ❑ Adequate restrooms for the number of students and staff
- ❑ Adequate play areas indoors
- ❑ Adequate napping facilities for those who require naps
- ❑ Sanitary procedures for food preparation
- ❑ Sanitary procedures for diaper changing areas
- ❑ A working fire alarm system
- ❑ Back up lights for power failures
- ❑ Ample parking for incoming and outgoing traffic
- ❑ Correct paperwork for all staff and children

A large center will be treated almost the same as a home child care center. If you do not pass the inspection the first time, any citations will be reported and returned to you via a list. Some items will be minor, and you are allowed to open as long as they are in the progress of being fixed within 30, 60, or 90 days. Major issues will need to be fixed before you are allowed to open.

The state will notify you when and if they will be re-inspecting your facility. If you have a tentative date set for opening, you will also need to have staffing ready. The paperwork must be up to date and accurate for each employee working under your direction. For each person's file, proof of a background check, physical examination proof filled out by a doctor, contact information, and social security number are required. Background checks must come back free and clear from the government before anyone is allowed to work at your center. Certain states may also require fingerprints or more specific information about every employee.

Fire Escape Plans

For all centers you will need to have a written fire escape plan. This plan is written out and details how you will escape if there is a fire. You will need to list the procedure for getting out, where you will go, and who you will contact. A fire drill should be practiced every month so everyone is familiar with the process should an emergency ever occur.

A written policy on discipline may also be required for your state. This policy states what actions may need disciplining action on your part. You also detail how and why you will discipline the child. The written policy is given to parents when the child registers so there is no misunderstanding on what happens when a child misbehaves.

Following is a sample graphic of what you will need to have prepared for a fire evacuation.

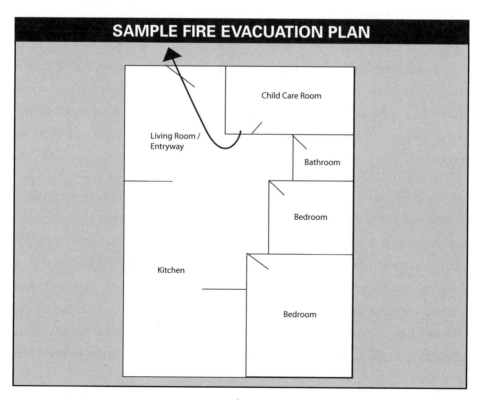

SAMPLE FIRE EVACUATION PLAN

Child Care Room

Living Room / Entryway

Bathroom

Bedroom

Kitchen

Bedroom

This shows a basic house layout, with the route from the main child care room to the front door. It should be followed with a written explanation of what will be done.

EXAMPLE WRITTEN PLAN

I will exit to the outdoors with all of the children. I will grab the emergency folder with the contact sheets and the first aid kit. I will then perform a role call to make sure everyone is present. I will proceed to a neighbor's house or use a cell phone to call 911. I will then notify the children's parents via cell phone or neighbor's phone and wait for the fire authorities to arrive.

HEALTH AND SAFETY POLICY

This policy may not be required by the government to operate, but it might be a smart idea to have one anyway. The health and safety policy will help keep the spread of germs and illnesses down, especially if you have a large center.

In your health and safety policy, you will want to include an employee sick policy. If the children are not allowed to attend with certain symptoms and illnesses, the staff should not be allowed to either. And when you make this policy, make sure to offer enough sick days for full time workers or unpaid days off for anyone who may need them without punishment, so they know you are serious about keeping healthy.

The sick policy for children can be the same for the staff: no fevers, no diarrhea, no vomiting, no undiagnosed rashes, or croupy coughs. If they are prescribed medicine, they should rest at home for at least 24 hours before returning. When they are diagnosed with highly contagious diseases, like strep throat, pneumonia, fifths disease, chicken pox, bronchitis, or anything else bacterial or viral, make them stay home for two days.

Your safety policy should also mention the importance of hand washing. Not only do employee's hands need to be washed after using the restroom, but they should be washed after close contact or body fluid contact with the children.

Washing hands after each diaper change is required. It is also required before any food handling at breakfast, snacks, or lunchtime. Make it a good practice to wash hands periodically throughout the day, regardless of what you may or may not have been in contact with.

Re-Inspection

After you have been approved for licensing and are open for operation, be prepared for an inspection at any time. Inspectors make unscheduled appearances on a routine basis throughout the year. They drop in unannounced to make sure that policies and practices are being followed, and they look for adequate staff to child ratios. If you are over your limit of how many children you are licensed for, you will be written up.

Inspectors also check to see if all the necessary paperwork is in order. They may look through all of the employee files and check for contact information. They will also look and make sure that all the necessary paperwork is filled out for every child. If the correct paperwork is not on file, you will need to get it quickly. The state can force you to halt care of a child until the paperwork is turned in, especially if it is the medical paperwork.

The inspector may also test the fire alarms and watch as you do a fire drill. They can also call a tornado drill and time you and the staff. If the drill appears unorganized, you may be written up for lack of training.

The inspector also has the right to examine any equipment for wear and tear in the indoor and outdoor play areas. Toys that are broken or in need of repair are discarded or removed. If the majority of toys and equipment appear to need repairs, a warning is given. You will have a set amount of days to replace the broken items or repair them to meet safety specifications.

All offenses are kept in your file with the state. If you get too many warnings and offenses against you or your center, your license will be in jeopardy. You could be placed on probation if your violations are minor. If you have major violations, like staffing issues or severely dilapidated conditions, your license may be revoked. Once your license is revoked, it will be very difficult to get another one.

Since each state has a different set of rules enforced by their governing body, be sure to check them before making any plans to open. Local municipalities may also have rules for zoning and what can happen within those zones. An in home center may be considered a business and not allowed in a residential setting. Check the resource guide at the end of the book to get your specific state's requirements or where you can go to get them.

After you go through the whole process of paperwork, inspection, and licensing, your license is good for a set number of years. Some states allow one, two, or three years to pass before you have to go through the whole process again. Sometimes the length of the license depends on the size of your center.

"While we try to teach our children all about life,

Our children teach us what life is all about."

~ Angela Schwindt

Part 2

Getting

Started

Now it is time to really get down to business. Where will you open? What should you name your business? What financing options are available to you? Do you want to run a specialized program? Is your house easily accessible from multiple towns?

All these facets are fun to plan. They need to be well thought out and planned in order for your business to be successful and well organized. If your business is poorly planned, getting started on the wrong foot can lead to a disaster down the road.

Much of the work for your successful business is done during the start up and initial phases of opening. You will need to be active in recruiting quality staff, clients to care for, marketing, and promoting your business to the community and surrounding areas.

In this section, all the basics from location to layout to marketing and advertising are discussed in detail. Use as much or as little information as you need to get your child care business off to a great start.

3
START UP EXPENSES & FUNDING

You really have your heart set on opening a child care center, but how much will it cost you? In reality, you can start a small, basic in home child care center for very little money. You will have the cost of food, which can be offset by reimbursement from a food program, toys, and supplies, which you may already have, office supplies, and licensing fees.

The true cost of beginning a child care center in your home could be under $500. Here is a sample list of the expenses before start up:

SAMPLE LIST OF START UP EXPENSES	
Licensing for in home child care center for six children	$125
Food for one week for six children (lunch, p.m. snack)	$ 45
Ad in newspaper classifieds to generate business	$ 25
Craft project supplies (one week)	$ 10
Bedding for naps	$ 60
Toys (if you do not have any go to garage sales)	$100
Office supplies (ledger book, receipt book, paper, stapler)	$ 50
	$415

To build on more toys and equipment, you can buy as you grow your business. As your business ages and expands, you will need to add more toys, replace old equipment, and modernize older equipment.

Start up expenses for large child care centers can add up fast, especially when you are buying everything new. When purchasing for a large or franchise center, you will require:

- Toys
- Art Supplies
- Office Supplies
- Staff Materials
- Chairs and Tables

- Baby Supplies – diapers, formula
- Food
- Kitchen Utensils
- Playground Equipment
- Cleaning Supplies

A large center caring for 125 children can expect to have the following expenses:

LARGE CHILD CARE CENTER EXPENSES	
License	$ 300
Food for one week	$ 1200+, depending on food
Newspaper advertising	$ 100
Craft project supplies	$ 100
Cots for naps	$ 2500
Toys	$ 4000
Office supplies and computer	$ 3500
	$11,700

The major expenses in running a large center are incurred from wages, insurance, outdoor equipment, and rent. If you have 125 kids ranging in age from birth to five years old, you will need a minimum of 15 people working full time to provide adequate ratios. Fifteen people working full time at the minimum wage (computed at the projected minimum wage rate hike for 2007) of $7.50 is a lot of money, and not all of your hours will be covered. If you open at 6:30 a.m. and remain open until 6 p.m., that is an 11 ½ hour shift. You will need two shifts or part-time employees to cover the overflow.

WEEKLY EMPLOYEE PAY ESTIMATE
15 employees @ $7.50/hour = $112.50 each hour
15 employees @ $7.50/hour = $112.50 x 40 hours = $4,500 in salary for one week

In addition to that number, you need to factor in the costs of any benefits you offer your employees. Do they get insurance? Do they get free or reduced rates for their own children attending the center? And on top of that, you need the expense of part-time employees and your salary. Staffing easily runs $6,000 per week in a large center.

Other major expenses for start up will be purchasing playground equipment. The new, modern play sets are large and plastic and installed on rubber surfaces. These play sets are designed for specific age groups and are very safe. However, a standard, no frills set with installation starts at $25,000 and can be over $100,000 for elaborate systems.

You can begin small with the outdoor equipment and build as you go and grow.

Every business starting out will need at least a little bit of seed money, no matter how frugal and careful you are in your spending. Whether the money is to purchase supplies or have capital on hand for payroll, money makes every business function. The amount of money you need to open will depend on the type of child care center you operate. Will you be able to personally fund all of the money required? Will you be able to get a loan or have to find personal investors to do so?

There are several ways to get financing for a business. You can look to government grants, funding by a silent or active partner, or financing by a sponsor or group. They all have pros and cons that will need to be investigated to see what works best for you. Before you go after any financing, you need a business plan.

Business Plans

When you are seeking financing, you will need to have a written business plan. A business plan is an in-depth report on what your business is, who your competition is, and how you plan to operate your business. The business plan will probably be required by any bank in which you are applying for a loan or any potential partners or investors whom you are seeking financing from.

A business plan needs to be well written and well researched. If you have no idea where to start, you can seek information from the library. There are many instructional books on writing business plans and what the contents of one should be. The books detail everything you need in order to present a strong, structured, and detailed business plan.

Another resource is any regional small business association. These are usually government funded agencies that help small businesses succeed. They not only help with business plan writing, they can help you find locations for funding. Small business associations also provide education on all of the ins and outs of business ownership, state tax requirements, and staffing requirements.

The length of the business plan will depend on how large a facility you are building and how much money you are requesting. There is not a set page count, but it needs to be well thought out and presented for approval.

The following items should be discussed in detail in your plan:

- Start up budget
- Operational budget

- Marketing plan
- Attendance goals
- Staffing needs
- Profit goals
- Your business policies, including discipline, emergency, disease prevention, safety

Other items that can be discussed in minor detail is the programs you will teach, optional services you plan on offering, the hours you will be open, payment schedules, holiday hours, employee discipline and termination, equipment needed, and the food you plan on serving.

The more information, the better with any business plan presentation. The more thought you put into your business and how it will run shows the financers how far you are willing to go to make it a success. A sloppy, poorly written business plan is a reflection of how you will run your business.

If you do not know how to write, hire a writer. Writers can create a solid and professional business plan for you with the basic details. See the resource section on where to find freelance writers. Only after a solid business plan is written should you seek financing from outside sources.

BUSINESS STRUCTURE

In conjunction with your business plan, you need to consider what type of structure you plan on opening. If you are planning on or have already opened an in home child care center, you may have not even known you were following a structure. The structure of your business organization will provide you with certain protections and responsibilities.

Sole Proprietor

This means your name and your name alone will be attached to the business. All correspondence, checks received, and checks issued will be to or from you. If you are an in home center, you may want to consider adding a spouse to your business for legal reasons. For instance, if you were to be hurt in an accident or become incapacitated, your spouse could make any payments or deposit any checks that came in during your absence. If you do not have a spouse, but want someone else to be responsible if you cannot be, forming a partnership may be beneficial.

A sole proprietor is the decision maker and the board of directors, all in one. You will report to no one, make decisions about all business operations, and make any changes to the business that you see fit with no approval needed.

Sole proprietors are usually home-based or small businesses. Since the government is trying to foster an environment in which small businesses can grow, survive, and thrive, they have many tax benefits. Tax benefits are created to make the incoming money go further. Child care centers benefit greatly because there are always expenses of food, supplies, equipment, and programming materials that are always needed. Whatever tax benefit you can qualify for will stretch your dollar further.

Partnership

A partnership involves going into business with one or more person. You have a partnership agreement or a contract written out, which details each person's involvement in the child care business. Not all partners need to be active in running the business, and some may be considered a silent partner.

Say you have three people who formed a partnership. One person is in charge of operating the center and managing the day to day operations. Another person is strictly working in the office, managing the books, payroll, and the ordering of supplies. The third partner is a silent partner, and does not want to run the business or be bothered with decision making questions. The third partner is a partner because they have probably invested money in the start up fund for the business. All the partners will split the profits from the center, no matter what their role is.

Corporation

A corporation is a business that is owned by a group of people who are all shareholders. A shareholder owns stock in your company, thus the company will be publicly owned. Each shareholder may own a different number of stocks or stock options, but they each have a vote in large business decisions. A really large corporation will have a board of directors, which heads the direction of the business.

Corporations in the child care industry are usually reserved for very large child care centers or a franchise. The positive aspect of forming a corporation is that you have a lot of protection under your corporate heading. The company would be sued, not you individually. It is not to say you could not be sued for civil infractions, but the corporation would head off any legal troubles.

Limited Liability Corporation (LLC)

A Limited Liability Corporation provides you with benefits similar to those of a sole proprietorship and a corporation. Under the LLC, you will be given as many tax breaks as you would under a sole proprietor business. LLCs are typically small businesses, or a conglomerate of small businesses, and can use any tax break possible. A LLC will also garner as much protection from liability, due to an accident, injury, or lawsuit, as a corporation has.

Each state has its own governing rules about LLC creation. One state may require a LLC have less than 15 employees, while another state may not have a rule for this. The fees associated with LLC ownership will also vary. The average rate for applying for a LLC costs a few hundred dollars, but can range from $100 to $1,200.

To get your business to LLC status, you can do it yourself. There are Web sites where you can purchase the paperwork and then print it out. To become a LLC, there is an application to fill out, a fee to pay, and a waiting period. You do not need a lawyer to process your paperwork or write up a contract. It can all be done on your own, and be perfectly legal for much less money.

LOANS

The most popular type of funding is taking out a loan. If you are taking out a business loan, there may be several options for interest rates and the term length. Make sure to thoroughly investigate every option. Apply at several different banks and credit unions; make the banks compete for your business.

There will be different term lengths, different interest rates, and different payment plan schedules. They can be tailored to fit your needs, too.

GRANTS

Another type of financing is grants. Grants are monies given by the government or a business that do not need to be repaid. Many philanthropic organizations also award grants for certain groups or business types. Grants have an extensive application process, just like a loan. There are applications to be filled out, and they often require in-depth information like a business plan would. If you do not have the time or wherewithal to find and write a grant, grant writers are available. The small business association is also a great resource for finding grants and how to obtain them. There are books at the library that list all of the places where you can apply for grant money.

Grants are usually available under a bunch of different categories. Hundreds of millions of dollars are given out every year. Grants are awarded to minority business owners, women business owners, business owners in low economic areas, and businesses who serve minorities. The possibilities are extensive, and to find the most available money you will need some assistance.

PRIVATE INVESTORS

Finding private investors is tricky. On one hand, you want to be in charge of your business and run it all by yourself, but you just do not have the capital needed to get off the ground. Finding outside investors may be the key if you do not want to or cannot get a bank loan. Private investors can be a silent partner or part of a group that make all of the decisions regarding your business.

To find a private investor, you need to use your contacts. Is there a local businessperson who invests in other business? Do you have a friend or relative that finances business and would help you out? If you do not know of someone to ask, take it to the small business association. This local resource might be able to connect you with the name or names of individuals or groups that invest professionally.

The Pros of Private Investors

- There is no note from the bank collecting interest.
- The money is up front.

The Cons of Private Investing

- You may give up a portion of control. A board of directors may want to decide on the business policies and have an active voice in the day to day operations.
- To get approval from the investors, you will also need to present your business plan. They may want changes made to your plan before they agree to hand over the money to you. They may

also require a say in your day to day operations. You will need to consider all of the concessions before you agree to take any money.

FAMILY AND FRIENDS

There is a saying that warns against borrowing money from friends or relatives. However, you may know someone who has business smarts, making it a positive option for you. And just because you are friends or share the same DNA does not mean you should bypass other standard procedures. Present a business plan, agree to the terms, and sign contracts for everything so expectations are very clear to everyone involved. A word of caution: Business partners are easier to walk away from if there is a dispute or the business does not succeed than family members are.

SBA (SMALL BUSINESS ASSOCIATION)

Not only does an SBA give you resources to run your business, they may also provide the financing. SBAs give out small loans to businesses that are just starting out. An SBA will also need a business plan to see what your goals and needs are.

CORPORATIONS

The corporation's aspect to opening a child care center may surprise you. Are there any large corporations in your town or a neighboring city that could benefit from having an on-site child care center? A hospital? A manufacturing plant? An accounting firm?

These large corporations may not have thought about the benefits of on-site care for their employees' children. Not only would you be providing a service to the families, but also the corporation would provide the funding and maybe even the location for your child care center. Present a plan for them that states all the benefits to their business and their employees, as well as how you can deliver those benefits.

The benefits of an on-site child care center:

- Employees can check on their children throughout the day

- Employees can share lunch with their child

- Employees are closer to their child if there is an illness or problem

- No lost hours because of employees calling in with no child care options

- Provide a backup for employees who use other child care methods that have a snag

CIVIC ORGANIZATIONS

Not only do corporations run child care centers, but non-profit and social agencies do, too. These agencies typically provide to low-income or minority families for a reduced or government aided fee. You can work side by side with the civic organization and provide care to children on their grounds. For example, the YMCA and YWCA usually run child care programs during the week and even on the weekend.

The civic organizations usually do not have an overflow of money to spare for start up expenses, so one or more of the above methods may be needed to get started.

Once you are approved for financing, you can begin planning. Put together all the next steps you will need to do and create a time frame for opening.

Maintaining Adequate Funding

Once your center is funded and operating, you need to make sure it continues to operate smoothly. One way to keep the cash flow in the black is by having a fundraiser each year, using the profits to make large purchases, buy big equipment for the children, or add a special program for them. Whatever you choose to do with the money, make sure it is something visible to the parents and children so they know the money was wisely spent. If you continue to have fundraisers where they do not see a benefit, participation will be lackluster. After all, the family is already paying you for services, why should they need to go out and raise funds for your center?

Another way to keep yourself well funded is by applying for grants. Grants are available at anytime during your business's operation, not just when you are seeking start up funds. There are different grants available for different niches. Do you care for a large percentage of minority children? Do you have several children with physical limitations? Do you provide a service for children after school and need transportation?

Finding a grant that fits your business is as easy as going online or looking in a book. Be careful who you enlist to help though. Some businesses will offer to help you search for grants, but they charge a fee. The fee could be a one time fee or a percentage of the grant you receive. Ask them up front what their fees include and get it in writing before you receive any help from them.

State and federal programming can also give your budget a boost. You may have to apply for it the same way you would a grant, but the process is not as hard and is worth it in the long run if you do not have to get a loan. State and federal programming dollars may come from being accredited, offering a specific service, such as before or after school care, or caring for children with a physical disability.

Once you have all of your financial ducks in a row, you can begin to plan and design your child care center.

CASE STUDY: KIM FARNES CORREA

The easiest part of opening up a daycare business, for me, was deciding that I wanted to be home for my son but at the same time earn an income. On the other hand, the hardest part was learning to make it professional. You are not just a mom – you are a businesswoman.

One tip that saved me from many headaches was to visit with daycare providers during their business hours before starting out. I observed for about an hour, letting them know what my intentions were up front. They were more than willing to share their contracts with me; I used them to tailor my own individual business contract. Many times I have had to refer back to my contract when difficult decisions needed to be made. A contract will take most of the emotion out of a difficult decision. However, I wish that I had known, before I started, that having a daily routine is crucial, not only for the children, but for your sanity.

I found that it is important to pay close attention when deciding who you would like to work with (e.g. the interviewing process). Go with your gut. If you like them or not, your gut instinct is always right.

When starting your own daycare business, like any other business, there are trials and errors. Nobody, I feel, will get it right the first time, but these experiences will only make you a better provider. It is also important to observe a few daycare centers, making sure this is something you feel you can do. It does take a lot of patience to run a home daycare.

My best experience as a day care provider is when a child does something for the first time on their own, after much help from you as a teacher helping them learn that skill. The pride and joy on their little faces is priceless. I still to this day (after nine and a half years of being in business for myself) have to remind myself that this is my business. I set my own freedom, my own hours, and my own pay. It is a beautiful thing.

"Little girls are cute and small only to adults. To one another they are not cute. They are life-sized."

~ Margaret Atwood

4
THE BASICS

All businesses have basic requirements in order to operate and run smoothly. Some basics needed for a child care center are a great location, a developmentally, child friendly environment, and supplies to run the environment successfully. When these basics are met and there is money left over, you can elaborate or add more to make your business even friendlier or larger to accommodate more children.

LOCATION IS EVERYTHING

If you are building a new center, choosing the location is very important. You will want to be on a main road or one that is relatively simple to get to. A center four miles out of town on a dirt road will not be very convenient for families, especially when they are in a hurry before work and eager to get home. The land might be cheap, but it will not be beneficial to your business.

Investigate all your options before purchasing any land or signing a purchase agreement. Check that road maintenance will not be scheduled in the near future, as that could interfere with your business. And check with the local road commission to see what improvements you will needed to make in order to build on the site. Do you need curbs put in? Sidewalks? A water line? These are all additional expenses that could eliminate the feasibility of building your own child care center. Be informed before you start the process so you know all your potential expenses.

A home or existing child care center's location cannot be changed, but if it is between major towns or easy to get to, families might not care where you are. They want a smaller, more intimate setting for their child care center. If you are a larger center a little off the beaten path, explore the costs and rules related to placing advertising at the nearest major intersection. If you are running at full capacity for children, this may not even be a concern.

The Layout

If you are building a brand new center, you will need a floor plan. Check with your local and state laws for room dimension requirements, entrance ways, playground space required, and bathrooms. Things to consider when drawing up a floor plan include: sleeping space for the children, employee break rooms, bathroom facilities for children and adults that are separated, play space, kitchen space, office areas, entry ways, teacher workrooms, and storage areas all suitable for the number of children you will be serving.

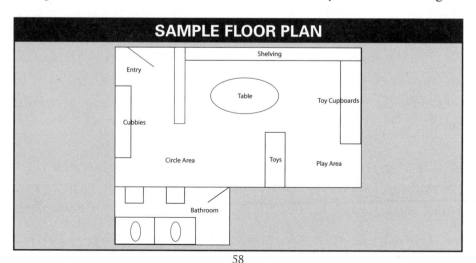

SAMPLE FLOOR PLAN

Besides the structure and size, you will need to meet the fire marshal's code. There will need to be smoke detectors, fire extinguishers, fire escape routes, and many other things to consider. All exit doors need to be open and easy to access.

With an established center, you may need to remodel or make sure it is up to code. The same may be true for your house. If you are using a basement strictly for your business, you will most likely need an egress window or walk out for adequate exit routes. A basement also needs adequate lighting and an exit sign that is lit up.

An existing building can be remodeled. You will need to ensure it is up to code, but it most likely is if it is in operation. Interrupting the day to day operations to remodel may be a pain for everyone involved. If shutting down for a short period of time is an option, you may want to consider it. However, you have to remember that every day you are shut down is revenue lost.

All types of centers will require a room large enough for children to play in. Shelves or storage bins to hold the toys can be placed along the walls to open up floor space for games, reading time, or even nap time. The rooms should be wide open, with an exit and ample storage space.

CUBBY DIAGRAM

Papers, Notes, etc.

Hats, mittens, change of clothes

Coats, jackets

Boots & shoes at bottom

To keep each child's belongings separate, a closet or cubby system should be used. Each child should have a closet or cubby space with a hook and space for a bag, boots, and other things. A separate closet room can even be used if you have a large number of children.

Cupboards with doors that shut can keep toys hidden when it is not playtime. You can also place important papers on top that need to be kept out of reach of little hands.

What to Call Your Child Care Center

You have the style of child care center, the location – now you need a name. You will want an appealing name and logo that represents who you are and what your business does. Are you a day school that offers preschool programs? Are you strictly a child care center? Incorporate your services in the title and when you do so, keep in mind what type of logo you want. Your logo will be on every ad and business material that leaves your building. Do you have a theme? Some examples of names would be Little People's Day School: They offer child care, preschool, and kindergarten programs; Woodview Terrace Preschool: The name of the street it is located on and they offer preschool programs; Judy's Home Child Care: The provider's name is Judy, and she runs the child care center from her house. Examples of themed day centers are Hundred Acre Woods, which uses all Winnie the Pooh and friends as decorations throughout the building. Each room is named after a certain character and decorated to match.

When you choose a name, make it as relevant and short as possible. You do not want a name like, The Teddy Bear Preschool Center on Smith's Crossing Road. It is a little wordy. Trying to fit that title on business cards may prove to be very difficult. It could be shortened to The Teddy Bear Preschool or the Smith's Crossing Preschool. And imagine answering the phone, time after time, and having to repeat the phrase. That may be your biggest factor in deciding on a shorter name.

Marketing and advertising experts will tell you to begin your name with the letter "A." That way, you will always be placed at the top of lists under child care providers, in the phone book, or even a Chamber of Commerce directory. For example, A-ONE Child Care will have people calling them if they advertise in any type of listing simply because they are at the top and the easiest to find. And they include exactly what they are, so there is no guesswork involved. A child care center with the name of Smith and Associates is far down the list, and gives an unclear view of what they do. They could be lawyers, doctors, or businesspeople. While you do not have to begin with an "A," pick something short that also describes your service.

Once you think you have a name for your business, you need to run several checks. First, check your local region to make sure someone has not already picked that name. Check the alphabetic phone book listings and then check under the child care section. If there is another business that happens to resemble your name, whether or not it is a child care center, you might want to change your name.

Second, search for legal availability on a larger level. This might mean you have to check state and federal sources for trademarked names. When your child care center is in Wisconsin and you want your center to be named the Mickey Mouse Club, you cannot do so because Disney has trademarked the Mickey Mouse Club, which prohibits anyone else from using it or any likeness of Mickey Mouse ears on their logo. This prevents a mix up with business accounts, mail, and any other businesses that try to use the same name.

Last, check the Internet. Run a search for the name you are thinking of using on the major engines like Google, Yahoo, and MSN. See if the domain name is available to create a Web site on. Say you want to have a child care center called Teddy Bears Child Care. Search under Teddy Bears Child Care and see what pops up. If someone already uses teddybearsdaycare.com, try variations. Is there a teddybears-daycare.com? Teddy-bearsdaycare.com? What about .biz?

When all three searches come back empty, meaning no one else is using that name, you are set to go. Fill out the paperwork to put the name in your business plan, the LLC application, and register a domain name. If you come up with a clever logo and tag line, you may even think of making it your trademark. Filing an application for a trademark can be done online for a fee. It will prevent others from using your design and logo.

Checking that no one else has your name, at least close by, will prevent unnecessary mix ups. When a different center in your area operates under a similar name, mail can be lost, tax and accounting records can be mixed up with the government, and your credit standing can be affected. If a business has a poor payment history or even bankruptcies in their history, it could inadvertently affect your financial standing. The simple solution is to make sure no one else is close to your name if they live within a few hundred miles of you.

Child Care Rates

Now that you have decided on a name and a location, it is time to make some money. Determining a fee to charge per child or per family may be very difficult. There are several things to consider, such as your overhead costs, how many, if any employees you need to pay, and what you would like your salary to be.

To begin, you need to decide how much you want to make. Find a realistic salary you would like to earn. Divide that number by 52 weeks, then by 40 hours. You can take the hourly rate and figure it out in a variety of ways.

Example:

You want to make $30,000 in one year.

30,000/52 weeks = $576.92/40 hours in a week = $14.40 per hour.

You need to figure out a way to make at least $14.40 per hour.

You can care for six children in your home without assistance. So, say you have five full time children (one is your own child) and opt to charge each one at $3.00 per hour. Then you are at $15 per hour, but only when all five children are there. That puts you at $120 per week, per child, but only if the child is in your care for 40 hours. Your day may end up being ten hours or $30 per day, per child. Then you need to figure in an additional fee per hour to make up for taxes, supplies, and food costs. The hourly rate would be more like $3.50 an hour, and at 50 hours, that is $175 for one child for one week. That price is a little high in most areas.

The Pros of Charging an Hourly Rate

- You are paid for the exact amount of care you are giving that child.

- Potentially you can earn more money with families who work long days.

The Cons of Charging an Hourly Rate

- The time it needs to keep track of hours arriving and hours leaving.

- Do you charge per full hour or ¼ hours?

- Disputes over hours if they are not written down right away or forgotten.

- Parents may send grandma or a friend to pick up the child to save some money (costing you money).

- You still need to factor in other expenses, such as taxes, supplies, and food.

- What do you do for sick days?

The cons seem to outweigh the positives of hourly care, so you should consider setting a weekly or flat rate per family.

Weekly Rates

Since charging an hourly rate for full or almost full time care of children may be difficult, a flat rate may work best for all involved. That way, no matter how little or how many hours the child attends, they pay one amount. A sick day, a holiday, or a vacation day can all be budgeted in to the flat rate, making the fee a fair amount for everyone.

When figuring out the flat rate, use the same table as for the hourly rate.

You want to make $14.40 per hour. Five children are in your care and average $3.00 an hour. Take 40 hours, multiply by 3.00 and get $120. How much food do they eat, how much supplies do they use, what are your overhead costs? A flat rate of $150 per child is a good rate to set.

In different parts of the country, rates are much higher or lower. For example, New Jersey child care centers can charge as much as $350 for one child per week. In northern Michigan, the average rate for one child full time is only $115 to $150. A rate of $250 for one child would be considered outrageous in Michigan, but very affordable in New Jersey.

The Pros of Charging a Weekly Rate

- You can plan your budget accordingly, since you know exactly how much money is coming in for the week and the month.

- You will still be paid when families take vacations and have sick days.

The Cons of Charging a Weekly Rate

- A family may be turned off if they need only four days of care, but will end up paying for five.

- You should figure out a system where you allow a family a set number of days or weeks where they can opt to not pay you. For example, you take two weeks off during the year. They can either pay you during these two weeks or opt to not pay you for two different weeks throughout the year. This way, they will believe they are still getting a deal since they are not paying for two weeks of vacation – whether it is yours or theirs – throughout the year.

- To check other child care rates in your area, call and investigate. Ask what they charge per child or per family. Ask if they distinguish between ages and have other fees for younger children. You can also visit your local state agency for childcare information and ask what the average rate is. They might not tell you exactly what a certain provider is charging, but they can give averages for your area. The differences can be vast within your own region. Keep your area in mind when you set the final price.

COMPETITION

When operating a child care center, no matter what your size is or where you are located, you will have some form of competition. It might be a large center with state of the art equipment. There may be several smaller, in home child care centers scattered across your town. You might even be competing with cheaper, non-licensed persons conducting child care out of their home. Competition is a fact of business operation and should be tackled as such. Competition happens and you need to deal with it positively and proactively so you can be on top. Make yourself be the top competitor in your area by offering exceptional services and outstanding quality childcare.

How Can You Compete Against a Fancy Day Care Center?

Just as easily as you can compete against a big one, a small one, or even a dumpy one. Choose your services, promote your businesses, charge a decent fee, and provide great quality care. Your satisfied families will help you promote yourself by word of mouth. And just because a child care center offers fancy services does not mean it is better. They may have fancy offerings, but bad hours of operation. Those fancy rates might also require higher fees. What you perceive as fancy competition may not be that to the families who will enlist your help. Not all families want the fancy services, but need the longer hours or affordability that you offer.

How Can You Compete Against Low Cost Day Care Centers?

First, find out if these centers are licensed. Chances are they are not. Unlicensed individuals will not have the licensing fees or requirements that you follow, giving them less overhead. Remind anyone who mentions that a competitor charges less that they will probably also be getting less: no meal requirements being met, no safety standards being watched, no discipline guidelines, and no state agency to monitor the child to adult ratios. While non-licensed people are not "evil and dirty," you need to be aware they are not licensed and remind potential families gently. Some families may see only the bottom line and not care about standards.

Like any athletic event, you do your best to win, but if you do not, you know you gave it your all. The same holds true for the business side of competition. Compete honestly and try to win business by promoting and advertising your services and rates. And chances are, if people do not end up coming to you, they would not have been a happy union with your current clientele. Things will always work out in the end if you try hard.

CASE STUDY: JANET CRISMAN

The easiest part of opening my business was finding the location. However, the hardest part was trying to find qualified teachers and retaining them. Before I started my own business, I wish I had known that there are so many people who will give you the right answers to your questions when you are interviewing them and then they just do not work out.

We started to have new staff and teachers work a week before we would put them on the permanent payroll. It worked out wonderfully and has continued to do so until this day. One tip that has saved me many headaches is that communication is the key part of supervision of staff and an essential part of partnership with parents.

I found that it is important to pay close attention to the staff. The staff needs to stay motivated and current on every level. They need to stay positive and have the right attitude to work with young minds. I also learned that, if you feel that someone is not going to work with your team, it is better to have to have him or her leave at the onset instead of letting the person cause a breakdown in the staff team. You should also stay away from parents that come to your center over and over and you just cannot satisfy them. It is better to cut your losses early and move on. It can cause so much tension in your staff if they have to deal with unsatisfied, difficult parents on a regular basis.

If you are going into business, make sure you read as much as you can. Find a mentor and pick his or her brain. Experience is a great asset. You should also find a qualified person to take care of the financial end of the business so that, as an administrator, you do not have to deal with that part of the business. You are so busy with parents, children, curriculum, guidelines, and staff that you do not need to have finances be a daily concern.

When it comes to forms, each state has its own required forms and not

CASE STUDY: JANET CRISMAN

everyone is familiar with them. I also think that observation forms are great and should be used more often. There was one center I worked with that could not afford to use them because it was a small, church-based center, and I felt the children were not really as easy to monitor as when you are able to track all the information from class to class.

My best experience as a child care provider involved a student I had when I first started working in the business. She was a little "pill:" She was always causing problems, but she had wonderful, supportive parents. She graduated and came back to work for us and is a wonderful and creative teacher. However, the thing that has surprised me most about being a business owner is that clients expect you to work from sun up to sun down.

Janet Crisman graduated from Luther College with a degree in music and business. She received her Masters in Early Childhood Administration from Wheelock College. Janet is married and has three sons. Crisman Consulting, which she owns with her husband Steve, provides growth and feasibility studies for nonprofit organizations, consulting for early childhood education programs, and "dress for success" consulting.

Janet Crisman – Owner, Crisman Consulting
248 Madera Way
Abilene, TX 79602
325-201-0195
Crisman5consulting@swbell.net

ABC

5
FEDERAL & STATE REQUIREMENTS

Most of the requirements you will need to meet to open and operate your business are state enforced. The state you live in controls how many children you are licensed to care for, how much training you and every member of your staff will need to complete, and what your building codes are. When you apply for your license, you send it in to your state office, not a federal one. They will continue to monitor your business during its longevity.

The federal branch of the government sets up the rules for IRS reporting and taxes. You can write a lot of your business expenses off for a home child care center, but you need to have the correct forms to do so. The IRS also has a special form that you fill out at the end of the year for your yearly income tax reporting. For large centers, the taxes are much more complicated and you should seek a tax advisor to make sure they are taken care of correctly.

INSURANCE

It may not be specifically required by your state, but insurance will be one of your greatest overhead costs. There will be several types of insurance policies you can take out to protect yourself, such as structural, liability, accident, and, if you have employees, health insurance and worker's compensation. While all may not be required to open and operate your business, they may be a smart decision and could save you a lot of money in the future.

If you run a child care center out of your home, your homeowner's insurance will cover your structure. You may want to check with your agent and see about adding a rider on to cover any equipment or supplies that go above and beyond what homeowner's might cover.

The state you live in may not require you to have liability insurance to operate. As a business owner, however, it would be a smart idea to protect yourself. The liability insurance will cover you for whatever amount you have set forth in your policy if you are sued for damages. Liability insurance will cover accidents, pet accidents, injuries with the child, damage to your property or theirs.

SANITATION

Since disease can become widespread quickly in a child care center, the state has set up guidelines for sanitation procedures. These procedures are fairly simple and straightforward, but need to be followed.

Diaper areas should be a flat, plastic or vinyl covered surface. After each diaper change, the surface needs to be sprayed with a bleach and water mixture. Then, a paper towel is used to dry off the surface and is discarded. This process must be repeated after each diaper change, no matter if only one child uses the diaper changing area. Many diseases and germs are spread through fecal contact, and the bleach reduces and eliminates most of them.

Sanitation around food preparation is also very important. Any table surface where snacks or meals are served needs to be cleaned daily with a three step method. Right before serving the snack or meal, the table should be sprayed with a soapy water mixture and wiped up. Then, plain water should be sprayed over the table and wiped. Last, a water and bleach mixture should be sprayed over the tables and air dried or wiped down.

In the kitchen, all cooking utensils should be washed with hot water and soap. All countertops where food is prepared should be cleaned using the three step method of soap, water, and then a bleach spray.

DAILY SCHEDULE

Some states even go as far as setting up daily schedule restrictions. The children may only watch so many hours of television per day. They cannot watch any shows that are rated PG-13 or higher. They cannot play outside unsupervised. Some of these are common sense, but they are spelled out so there is no error on the provider's part.

Check your state out carefully and see if you can abide by all the rules. No matter how silly some of them sound, they need to be followed in order to have your licensing upheld. If you are reported for violating any of their policies or rules, you can quickly lose your license to operate.

FOOD PROGRAMS

If your state offers a food program, belonging to it is usually voluntary. Belonging to the food program is a huge benefit to you. The food program is a state agency that monitors the food you feed the children. When following their program, you are reimbursed a certain percentage of the cost of the food each month. The state requires certain foods to be served daily, like fruits and vegetables. They also monitor what snacks are fed to the children. Menus will need to be kept each day and sent in at the end of the month in order for you to receive payment.

If the menus are not followed, your money will be cut or suspended. A food program person will routinely inspect your premises, announced and un-announced, to make sure you are following procedures.

IRS REQUIREMENTS

As with any business, the IRS will want their share. Meticulous records will need to be kept of all financials, no matter what size of child care center you open. Accurate reporting and detailed financial ledgers will make tax reporting go much smoother.

Tax Reporting

In order to be a licensed provider, you will need an EIN. This is an Employee Identification Number, and it is used for your income tax reporting. With an EIN, you claim your income to the government. The families that you care for can also claim the money they pay you and get a tax credit for some or all of it.

The government taxes your income like any other small business, so you will probably need to pay in at year's end or pay quarterly installments so the total at the end of the year is not so high. Keep track of all of your receipts, business expenses, and license expenditures that can be written off. If you are a home child care provider, you can get a portion of your electricity, water, garbage, and other expenses written off each year.

Write Offs

In your home, measure what size area is used for child care. Get the square footage of that area and figure out what percentage it is of your total square footage. Do you use 50 percent of your house for child care activities? Then you can use a formula created to account for depreciation.

Electricity can also be written off in portions, as well as any water, Internet, cable, phone, and garbage services. An accountant who specializes in business tax reporting will know the ins and outs of what you can and cannot deduct.

Purchases of toys, craft supplies, and outdoor equipment can be written off in part, even if they were meant for or are used by your own children. No matter how small you think an item is, keep the receipt. You may be surprised at how much those little purchases add up.

"Children are unpredictable. You never know what inconsistency they're going to catch you in next."
~ *Franklin P. Jones*

6
BUSINESS NEEDS

Your business will have several needs before it can open.

FINDING STAFF

A business cannot run itself. There needs to be at least one person on the helm. That person usually needs some type of equipment or supplies to do their job properly. Even a small home center will need adequate supplies to run smoothly.

The most vital aspect of a business is its employees. Without staffing, nothing would be accomplished. Even if you are the highest paid CEO of the most profitable company, your employees help you get there every day. Remembering that in your day to day operations will create respect and understanding on both sides of the coin.

The amount of staff you will need to run a child care center depends upon how many children you are licensed for. If you operate in your home with six children, you can handle the deed by yourself. It may be a good idea to have an assistant or emergency person to contact when something comes up unexpectedly. An assistant can step in and care for the kids if you have a doctor's appointment or if one of your children becomes sick, and you cannot care for the other children. An assistant will also come in handy if you need a vacation or sick day.

A large center will need staffing based on its enrollment. The state the center is in determines how many adults are needed for a group of children by the age. Infants under 18 months old need one adult per every three infants. For every four children between ages 18 months and three years there needs to be one adult, and one adult can care for six three-year-olds. Four-years-olds require eight children per every one adult. Five-year-olds and older can have 10 children for every one adult in the room.

Hiring

Choosing your staff is hard work. The first step is determining where to advertise. The newspaper will provide the most exposure, but it will probably also bring in a larger number of unqualified applicants. Screening applicants is a long and tedious process. By targeting your advertising to a larger pool of qualified people, you will eliminate unnecessary screening time.

Places to advertise job openings may be in a college newspaper with a large education program. College students studying education may have a flexible schedule and the desire for part-time jobs.

Another place to advertise is in a program that offers childcare training to high school students. These students are not the traditional "college prep" students, but are those who have other interests besides high academics. Alternative schools often provide co-ops to students who work in childcare settings. These students are more than capable of caring for children; however, they are not old enough to be licensed on their own.

When taking applications for staff, have them send as much information as possible. Request a résumé and references along with a cover letter stating their interest. Having this information up front is important for several reasons. First, you can save a lot of time by scanning their résumé; this will tell you how much experience they have.

Second, if a candidate has potential, you can verify employment and references before you schedule an interview. By talking with their references, you can gauge their potential.

Third, if you get many good candidates but only have a limited number of positions open, you can compare their application packets side by side. Does one résumé have a lot of spelling mistakes and grammar errors? Is one cover letter written completely wrong and full of errors?

However much information you can garner ahead of time will save you time in the interview process. If you simply interview everyone who applies, you may be wasting several days or hours with people who are not qualified.

Interviewing

After you have a stack of potential candidates, set up interviews with each of them. During the interview, take as many notes as possible so you can review the information later. If you have many interviews in a short period of time, the information can become jumbled and you may confuse the candidates.

Ask pointed questions during the interview. After all, these people will be caring for young children that you will ultimately be responsible for. Ask what their goals are for the future. What do they like most about working with children on a daily basis? What are their beliefs on discipline?

If the candidate has the "right" answers and enough experience, put them on an "approval" status. They need to submit to a background check before they are allowed to work with children. To get the background check, they will need to be informed of your intent. You can get permission for a background check in one of two ways. You can inform them they are a top candidate, but you need to have a background check done. They need to authorize a consent form and provide a social security number for you to receive the background check information. Another way to get authorization is to tell them you have other people to interview, but in order to make a decision you have to conduct a background check.

The background checks of those that are hired need to be kept on file. If you decide to offer transportation services, you may want to check the driving records of your staff. Your insurance will also take those driving records in to consideration, which may cost you additional premiums.

See a sample questionnaire to ask during your employee interview in the resource section.

Benefits and Pay

Besides determining your own salary, setting wages for your employees may be one of the most difficult tasks. You will need to pay at least minimum wage, which is on the rise for 2007. Some states are already higher than others, but a safe budget is $7.50 per hour.

Some things to take into consideration when coming to a reasonable dollar per hour figure include skills. Does this person have exceptional experience working with children and require little or no supervision from you? Do they have a degree? Have they run an in home center before? These may all be situations where you can increase their pay. Raises can always be given to employees as they continue to work for you.

In addition to pay, you might want to consider the benefits you can offer your employees. Usually only large centers and franchises can offer a complete benefits package with insurance, 401(k), and vacation time. If you are a small to medium sized center, there are a few perks you can offer to your employees that do not cost as much as insurance and other traditional benefits.

One hot item to offer would be free child care for up to two of their children. How nice is it to be out of your house and working, yet still be in the same place as your children?

Another benefit would be to provide lunch to your staff. Someone is cooking for the children, so why not feed the caregivers, too? Just offering means you can claim it as a benefit to the job you are offering them.

Orientation

Having an orientation period at the onset of employment, often the last step in the hiring process, may be used in several ways. A person has made it through the interview and is willing to work for you. To make sure they will be a good fit, offer to pay them to come in for half a day. That way, they can get a good idea of what they will be doing every day. Saying what the job is like in an interview may be different from the actual job. An orientation will eliminate any myths about their responsibilities. Having an orientation will also give you a glimpse into their abilities. They may have said they worked with four-year-olds for three years, but if they appear confused and unsure of themselves after three hours in a preschool room, you know they were fibbing in the interview. If the orientation works well, you can officially hire the person.

An orientation can also be the first part of the training process. A person will come in and spend a day or two with you before being placed in their designated classroom for hands on training. In this orientation, they can fill out any necessary forms, watch any training videos, and get a feel for the center. They can be given a folder with all your policies and procedures and given time to read and study them. They can also meet the other staff members and have a tour of the facility.

Training

If an employee has worked in a child care setting before, chances are they will need little training. The only training they may need is in the specific processes in your center. Some employees may need a little more training. For example, a person might have worked in a child care center previously, but in a room with four-year-olds. Now they are placed in a room with toddlers, and it is completely different. They have adequate experience with children, but only with a certain age. Getting them acclimated to a different age group will take minimal time and a little guidance.

Training your staff in other areas will be a constant process. Your state may require a certain amount of hours per month or per year in child development training per employee. These classes can be offered through you and can include topics like health practices, development, or bettering their skills. Other options may be taking classes through a local community college. The classes will have a minimal fee.

Agencies that work with childcare providers also offer night and weekend classes. The classes may be more specific and targeted to certain aspects of child development, handling problems in your business, or diagnosing a problem with a child or their family.

CPR

CPR (Cardio Pulmonary Resuscitation) and first aid certification will be required for all employees in some states. This certification is usually offered through the Red Cross, but may be acceptable by other instructors in the medical and health fields. Participants must pay to cover the certification and instruction fees.

CPR is beneficial because it covers all breathing emergencies. It will teach your staff how to handle choking, heart stoppages, and blocked airways.

Expectations

Just as your business needs a direction, any and all employees need the same guidance. Upon joining your child care center, give your new employees a complete job description. List all of their job responsibilities and how you expect them to be performed. Some samples of expectations may look like this:

- Arrive on time every shift

- Be courteous and friendly to all parents and children

- Perform bathroom cleaning duties each morning

- Assist with getting children on and off the bus daily

- Help prepare breakfast daily

- Wash the dishes after the afternoon snack time

Set up a period of time where you will review their performance. It may be after the first 90 days, it may be every six months, or it could be an annual process. Make it consistent, and be reliable about performing the employee reviews. Employees generally like to receive feedback and know that they are doing their job correctly. If you have a large enough revenue intake or budget, you may even consider a reward system for consistently high reviews.

When an employee is not meeting expectations, a review system gives them a constructive way to improve and better themselves.

Substance Policy

Even though such things should be clear, you need to have a substance policy written and posted for your staff. This policy should state that absolutely no illegal drugs or alcohol will be tolerated on the child care premises. If such substances are found during business hours (you may need to allow wiggle room here if you have holiday parties with alcohol on the premises) it is grounds for dismissal.

You may even want to consider including tobacco products, including chewing tobacco, cigars, and cigarettes, in this policy. When you make the decision to forbid tobacco products on your grounds, that means parents are not allowed to do so either. Employees may smoke in their own cars while on break, but not outside the kitchen door.

Staff Meetings

To keep a large center in tune with each other, a monthly staff meeting might be a great idea. Getting everyone to attend may prove very tricky, however. You might be able to schedule the meeting early, when some of the staff is reporting and before a lot of children arrive. Ask (or pay) the other staff to come in early. You could also do this towards the end of the day, when most children have left with their parents.

A staff meeting does not have to be a stiff, formal affair. It can simply be a place where any concerns or problems between staff members, with children, or with the center are raised. Some of the best input will come from those who work for you. The staff meetings can also be a place to discuss upcoming events and share recognition.

Rewards and Recognition

Everyone deserves a pat on the back, especially care givers who work with children. Awards and recognition breed further excellence in standards. To get and give appropriate recognition to yourself and your staff members, you can do several things.

Holiday Parties

Who does not enjoy a holiday party? If you cannot forget about being politically correct, alter your parties. Make it the year end celebration instead of Christmas party. Call it the winter season celebration, but still give presents to each other.

When you are not worried about being politically correct, host a holiday party for your staff and their spouses or significant others. When your center pays for the expense, or a majority of it, try and plan a less extravagant affair. Opt for a potluck dinner. The center can provide the paper products and the dessert. Give each person a token of appreciation. It does not have to be something extravagant, like $100 gift certificates to a spa, but a small gift certificate to a bookstore would be nice. When employees are recognized and know they are appreciated, they will perform even better and remain loyal to you.

Awards

There are two ways to go about handing out awards. You can make them fun or you can make them serious. The serious awards could include:

- Most Training Hours in a Year
- Best Implementation of Educational Program
- Employee of the Month
- Budget Underachiever

Some fun awards you can hand out monthly or yearly would include:

- Most Diapers Changed in One Day
- Best Use of Recycled Materials in a Craft Project
- Most Innovative Get to Sleep Trick
- Most Noses Wiped in an Hour

Print out certificates from the computer and have fun with the awards. Breaking out of the daily routine will keep everyone happy.

Recognize Years of Service

Reliable and trustworthy staff members are very hard to keep in the child care business. Turnover rates are traditionally very high, so when you have an employee who stays with you, reward that staying power. Each time they hit a milestone, honor them. If you are buying an existing center, you will need to go back through employee records and find the hire dates so you know when the anniversaries are.

Recognize Accomplishments

An accomplishment might not be something that happens inside the center. One of your employees may have received their associate's degree in childcare. Have a party to celebrate. If you honor them and show you appreciate their work, they may stay with you for years to come.

When your staff stays late on a Thursday so they can listen to disease prevention training, make sure your families know it. Mention in the monthly newsletter that the whole staff gave up their Thursday night for training on keeping the children healthy.

Promote Caregiver Appreciation Week

Every year there is a week to honor teachers and caregivers. Make the whole week a special affair at your child care center. Offer prizes and drawings for your staff via a nomination form. Set up a table at the entry way with slips of paper. Have the families nominate a staff member by recognizing a good deed they performed. Each day, pull a name out of that bucket and give the winner a prize.

Plan a special luncheon for the staff. You can have a lunch catered or maybe a parent would be willing to organize a lunch and have different families bring a dish to pass around. Either way, providing a nice lunch is a great symbol of recognition.

Even if you are at home, you can celebrate with your children. Hang up a sign and make cupcakes for everyone to eat. Small businesses deserve recognition, too.

Not every aspect of having employees is a pleasant one, no matter how hard you try. Following are ways to handle a "problem" staff member.

Firing

You have hired and trained a staff member. You have come to know them pretty well, but things just are not working out for any number of reasons. They have an absenteeism problem, they are continually sick, or worse, they are too harsh with discipline. Whatever the reason may be to terminate an employee, you will need a process to follow to do so.

Before you hire any staff, you should devise a plan for termination. That way, when they are hired they know the rules and what will happen if they are not followed. They may get one or two verbal warnings that are kept in their personnel file. Then, they may get one, two, or even three written warnings. The steps that lead up to termination are determined by you, but all employees need to be aware of what they are.

When an employee has gone through your written or verbal warning policy, they should be let go. You may do so verbally, but also follow it up in writing. Explain exactly why and when they were let go, and keep records of it if they ever try to come back and accuse you of wrongful dismissal.

MISCELLANEOUS "STAFF"

Not only will you need to have the obvious players in a large child care center, you may also want to think about having some minor players in your business.

Lawyer

A lawyer can review any policies you put in place. They can also look over the service contract and help with the terminology. They will not need to be consulted for every one, just the initial language on the blank form you will copy and have every family sign. The lawyer can also be on stand by if a problem arises from liability or employee disputes.

Accountant

This may be the most important person in your life. Not only can this person handle your entire payroll, billing, and receiving, but they can manage taxes, too. This may be the most important person you hire, even if it is only part-time. If your financial records are kept in good order, your business will run much more smoothly in the future.

Housekeeper

Who is going to clean up the place? The children and staff in each room can keep their room clean, but who will clean everything else? Will the staff take turns cleaning the bathroom and vacuuming the entryway? Probably not without a lot of grumbling.

Your center can hire a part-time janitor, but there may not be enough work to keep someone busy part time. There would be bathrooms to clean, floors to take care of, the office, and maybe a staff room. It may be cheaper, or more feasible, to hire a cleaning service that comes in once or twice a week to clean the windows, vacuum or mop the floors, take care of the trash, and tidy up the office.

Maintenance Man

A maintenance man can be in the form of a spouse or significant other in a home child care center. But what do you do in a large center that needs repairs, but not major ones? A part-time maintenance man might be the solution. A maintenance person can take care of any tasks around your building, on the inside and out and could also be responsible for the grounds keeping.

When you are a medium sized center and do not believe you require the services of a part-time maintenance person, you can enlist a maintenance service. These are companies you can call and give them a list of all the repairs you need done. They will charge an hourly rate to complete the projects.

Snow Removal

If you have a large parking lot, or opt not to hire a maintenance man, you will need someone to remove snow. Snow removers often work for several businesses and charge a per year fee for removing snow. You would set up a contract with them, and it would be a standing order that whenever there was, for example, two inches of snow or more, they would come and plow. If you sign a contract with them, you can be very specific about what you want.

Financial Planner

This person would function differently than an accountant. They can plan for your future, advising you where and when to spend profits. They can also suggest ways to capitalize on revenue generation. A financial planner usually charges a fee based on the amount of revenue they are working with. If they are strictly consulting with you, they may charge a flat fee. If they are managing money in mutual funds or stocks, they would charge a percentage of the value of that money.

IT

Technology will keep any business running smoothly. Whether you have one computer running accounting software or you are hooked up to a franchise mainframe, you need someone to call when you have problems. Computers are vital to the success of a business, and when one is not functioning, it may affect the business. The IT person may be in charge of your Web site, too.

An IT person can be strictly computer related, or it may be a person who encompasses all things technological, such as copiers, fax machines, media equipment, etc. An IT person can be called from a local electronics store and paid a service charge and consultant's fee. Ask about all fees and charges before you agree or you may be surprised by how much they charge per hour.

Business Consultant

A business consultant is a professional that helps steer your business. They can provide suggestions and determine a new route for you when you want to expand or change services. They can give advice on loans, financers, and grants. They know a lot about operating a business, whether it is large or small. A business consultant can be free from the local SBA or it can be a specialist you hire.

Marketing/Publicity Person

This person could be worth their weight in gold, too. If you do not have the time or the knowledge to craft words to your advantage, you should hire a marketing specialist. This person can write all your advertising, create your media kit, send out press releases, and write articles for the newspaper. They may charge a per word fee or provide services at an hourly or per project rate. They can not only create the words to sell your business, but they will know where to send them to get the most exposure for you.

You did not think there would be so many people required to run one business, did you? The good news is you will not need to have all of these people on board full time.

PLAY TIME

Once the staff is in place, the children will need something to do. Getting the right equipment ahead of time will make your center a fun place for the kids and enjoyable for the adults. In addition, the equipment is not just any equipment, but toys. What kind of a person does not like shopping for toys?

To properly choose toys for your home or center, keep in mind the age and sex of each group. Are your children all boys or all girls? If so, you may need to expand your selection. A room full of boys is not going to play with Barbie dolls until you can find some boy toys. Get a few good boy items, like trucks, trains, or cars, and they will be happy until you can add to the toy collection.

When there are multiple age brackets in your house, use toys that your own children used. If your children have grown past a stage and you got rid of those toys, scour the garage sales or ask friends if they have extra. Babies and toddlers do not require a lot of toys, but they do need safe toys that encourage and foster healthy development. Large blocks, soft toys, board books, and plush animals are great for young children to chew and play with. It is also important to keep in mind that, if you plan on shopping garage sales for toys, you consult a toy recall list in light of the recent recalls.

If you do not have a large budget to spend on updating and expanding your toy selection, try garage sales, second hand stores, and discount retailers. Often times, garage sales will have the best selection of toys since they are tried and true by the seller's own children. Sometimes the children at the garage sale still will not want to part with a favorite toy, even if they have out grown it. Then you know you have a winner on your hands. Check the toy over thoroughly for cracks or broken pieces to make sure it is safe. When a toy is part of a larger set, make sure it has all or most of the pieces. Some items will not require every original piece, like a dollhouse. Other toys, like a puzzle, need every piece or they are useless.

The best places to go for garage sales are neighborhoods that appear to have young children living in them. Like most families, they are overrun with toys and are just opting to get rid of some clutter in their homes. These toys are usually cheap and in great condition.

When garage sale shopping is not an option for you, head to the toy store. Before you shop, make a list of your preferred items for each age group. Buy an equal number of toys for each group so everyone has something new to play with and enjoy.

Your center will not open for a few weeks or even months, so you have some time to shop around and get the best prices. Keep an eye out for sales in the Sunday papers. Look around online and see if you can get even better deals. With the popularity of online shopping, many stores will offer free or discounted shipping, especially on purchases over a specified dollar amount. Certain educational outlets or children's equipment stores will give discounts to teachers and child care providers.

Cleaning Your Toys

When you live at home, with only your children, cleaning their toys may not be a top priority. However, when there are other children in the home using those toys, day after day, suddenly being germ free is appealing — and not to mention a good sanitary practice for keeping germs and sicknesses from spreading.

Infants and toddlers put everything in their mouths. When there are several infants and toddlers in your care, keep certain toys specific to each baby.

That way, day after day, the baby is chewing on their "own" toys and not spreading germs. If that is not an option, you will need to wash each toy every night by hand or in a dishwasher.

When children get older, the toys only require sanitization once a month unless there are flu bugs going around. Place the toys in mesh bags if they are little and place them on the top rack of the dishwasher. Allow the toys to thoroughly dry before putting them back in to play. When an outbreak has occurred, washing the plastic toys more frequently, like daily or weekly, may help to contain some of the germs. However, when children reach a certain age they should know not to put toys in their mouths. You can work this in to a lesson plan if you have continuous offenders.

Toys that cannot be put in a dishwasher or washed in a sink can still be cleaned. Use a mixture of diluted bleach water in a spray bottle and spray the object thoroughly. Some items needing a spray may include dollhouses, building sets, and large games. After the toy is sprayed, wipe it down and let it air dry completely before it is played with again.

Other toys that are frequently touched, such as stuffed animals, puzzles, or large objects are hard to disinfect. If these require disinfecting, from certain things such as head lice, they can be placed in a garbage bag and stuck in a freezer for 24 hours. Stuffed animals are hard to wash, but they can be put in the machine on the gentle cycle if absolutely necessary. Anything can be set outdoors in freezing weather and after a couple days, germs should be dead.

Storing Your Goods

One of the hardest things to manage when you run a child care center is the toys. Where do you store everything? How can you keep the rooms clean but still allow the kids to use their imagination and play skills to have fun?

At home child care centers, having a separate room for the children to spend the majority of their day will keep the toys out of the rest of your house. If your house is not big enough to have a separate room, use a living room or basement for your headquarters. Stack bins full of toys along a wall when they are finished playing. Keep their belongings in a closet or cubby with each child's name.

In your home, extra storage bins or shelving units can hold a variety of toys. Use separate bins in all sizes to sort toys. Draw a picture, tape a picture, or label each bin so that when the kids are cleaning up, they know what toy belongs in what bin. This will also make clean up time more efficient. Using small and separate bins for items will keep small pieces together.

In a center, space will be to your benefit. Bookshelves and cupboards can store bins of all sizes. You can even order special shelving units to store the toys and supplies needed for each room of your center.

Separate cupboards or closet organizers can be set up to keep all craft and art supplies separate and out of the hands of little ones. The high shelves can be used for things like paint and glue that could be a real mess if opened by the children. Any sharp items, like scissors, pins, tacks, and staples are also safest when kept up high or in a closed drawer or cupboard.

7
PROMOTING YOUR BUSINESS

GENERATING PUBLICITY

To promote yourself and your business, you can enlist the help of paid and unpaid forms of publicity. Some forms of paid publicity include advertising on radio and in the newspapers. Unpaid forms of publicity include press releases, articles, and certain marketing practices.

Some methods of attracting attention to your business can be high profile, such as a local television crew being live on site to watch a grand opening ribbon cutting ceremony. High profile campaigns for marketing and advertising are designed to draw widespread attention to your business. Often this attention is meant to drive up your business. Other times, it is to keep your name fresh in the minds of the community members.

Other methods of marketing can be low profile, such as a newsletter to families in your care. Low profile marketing and publicity is just as important, as it reaches out to people who already use your services and keeps them informed of your activities.

Marketing to Potential Clients

In order to have a successful child care center, you need to advertise and promote your services. If you are starting a new center, you will need to use each method to gain business. High profile advertising and marketing will net you the best results quickly. If you are purchasing an existing center, you may need only a couple marketing tools to gain new families.

What is the difference between advertising and marketing your business? Advertising is the actual print or audio script written to promote your business. The advertising is placed in newspapers, magazines, and possibly on the radio or TV. There are many other means for advertising, but these are the major ones. Marketing is promoting your business through a variety of paid and unpaid methods. Advertising is one part of a marketing plan.

Some marketing plans are very expensive, but you can also effectively market yourself and your business for little money. It just requires some planning and effort on your part.

Know What You Are Promoting

Before you can market or advertise anything, you need to know exactly what it is you are promoting. Start out your marketing campaign by writing a benefit statement. Make a list of your services, including hours of operation and any special programs or services offered. When you make any kind of ad, flyer, or brochure, you can reference this sheet to get ideas of what you should include. Not every place you advertise in will be long enough to hold all of them, but you can pick and choose what benefit will stand out most for that method. For example, you have a short radio spot scheduled for the late evening hours. In the ad, it would be smart to mention that you offer extended hours so that any parent listening at work during that time would say, "Hey, I need a child care center with those hours."

After you have a benefit statement, make copies of it. If you own a large center, keep one by each phone. That way, whenever a prospective family calls, this information will be at the fingertips of the person answering the phone.

ADVERTISING

Print

Print advertising goes much deeper than a blurb in the daily newspaper. There are many niche magazines, sponsored either by the daily news or another independent printer, that work great for child care center advertising. There are now papers that specialize in families and local events for specific regions. In their classified section, there will be a place for childcare centers and preschools. There are also themed sections in the newspaper that place advertisements. The fall issues usually focus on schools and related activities, and families looking for new child care center can find you easily.

Print advertising can also come in the form of a story in a newspaper. The new business you are operating may be a very newsworthy item, especially if your area has a shortage of child care centers. To attract attention to your opening, a press release should be sent to all the local news agencies, including radio stations, newspapers, and community organizations. (See the resource section for an example of a press release.) A press release is a one page letter that details what you are, what you offer, and where to go to get further information. To attract the most attention to your release, you will need to have a fun and interesting angle to it. If the news service that picks up the press release finds it interesting or unique enough, they may call you to do an in-depth interview or story. Any amount of recognition you can get, especially if it is free, will only boost your business. Even if you do not see families knocking down your door as soon as the story is run, the press is working. Your name is getting out around town and passed between families who may not have an immediate need, but will keep you in mind for future needs.

In short, print advertising can be found in:

- Phone books
- Newspapers
- Magazines
- Church bulletins
- Community bulletins

- Regional family magazines
- School newsletters
- High school newspapers
- Chamber of Commerce news
- Township or county newsletters

Miscellaneous Print

Other forms of print advertising might include creating a banner to hang outside of your building. Banners usually only have room for one or two lines, so be sure to put the space to good use. Use the name of your center at the top with a logo. On the second line, list an address, a phone number, and a Web site address, if it fits. This way, the banner can be hung outside of your house or building, but it can also be used in parades, at parenting fair booths, and at a sponsorship table.

Radio

The radio is another easy way to get your name in to the public forum. A short, 30 second ad aired during the right time slot can get you a lot of attention. In your ad, list your location, your hours, and if you have an open house or upcoming event. Give a phone number and a Web site where more information can be found.

A radio commercial can be created in a radio studio or at home on the computer. You do not need fancy programming, just a microphone and recording software. When you create your spoken ad, you can send the audio file to the radio station, and they can doctor the quality if it needs sprucing up. When you have a larger budget to work with, you can hire a marketing agency to write, create, and distribute your ad.

Online

Online advertising is done through your Web site or through ads you place online. You can use adwords and create a specific campaign to target an audience. Simply pick what keywords you want to be associated with. Child care centers, child care, preschool, and day care are all good keywords that will attract a lot of searches. You set a dollar amount to spend per month, and adwords will display your small, three- line ad on certain pages of Web search results. The ad is what you see in the right hand column or along the bottom of the search results page.

Your Web site is also a great way to advertise. When people are referred to your site through other means, via radio or print, they can get many more details. Make a section on the Web site just for potential clients. Give them lists of things your center does, what your schedule is, and who your employees are. Place lots of pictures of you and the children playing. Include a coupon that is good for a half-priced registration or 10 percent off their first month if they register online. Printing coupons online is free for you, but great for getting the attention of a potential client.

MARKETING

Marketing uses all of the above methods and others to make your business name remembered by people. Getting the word out is easy. Does your town have an annual festival? Is there a parade for homecoming or another school event? Do you have regional newspapers? Contacts with a TV station? Use everything at your disposal to create a buzz surrounding you and the business.

Parade

A parade float is a great way to get your name out. Entering a parade is usually free. Have a vehicle with your name on both sides for easy viewing. Gather a group of neighborhood children or children who are already in your service to join you. Have the children throw candy with a label attached to it. On the label, list your business name and phone number, or even a Web site.

You do not have to just throw candy either. Parents standing along the sides can get flyers or other snacks with a label on it. A pencil with the company name and logo will not break when it is thrown to the ground. Or you can really specialize, and hand out sample shampoo packets, hand lotion, or "spa" type products that moms like to use.

Make an Event

If you have an opening date scheduled at a large center, make it a grand opening. Have a large banner and balloons out front to draw attention to your location and your business. To coincide with the grand opening, a special press release may be needed to draw extra attention to that event, especially if you have something fun going on.

To make your grand opening fun, schedule a clown, a magician, or a local author to come and read. Offer something for free and encourage the public to come. When they come to check the performer out, even if they do not or might not think they need child care services, you are getting exposure. Have copies of your business flyers out so they can grab one or more for themselves. Chances are, if your new center looks warm and inviting, they will take several and place them in their office for others to see.

Market Yourself

In order to get business, you will need to promote yourself. People find it hard to do, but it must be done and done well to get the word out about your child care center. Even if you are an in home child care center, you will need to advertise. Whenever you get openings, you may also need to do a little advertising to bring in business.

One way to prepare for marketing is to create a media kit. A media kit has several tools in it that can be used for advertising, and it can include, but is not limited to, flyers, a press release, brochures, business cards, a video message or commercial, a sample of your menu, program, and daily routine, and the names and credits of all or any of your staff. The media kit items can be used together or separately as needed. It can even be put together in a folder and handed to media outlets such as a television station, a publisher, or a public relations person.

Business Cards

Print or have business cards printed for you. They simply need the business name, logo, and contact details. If room allows, place your hours on the bottom so clients can see a benefit of your services right away. A business card can be dropped in any contest at a restaurant or other place of business. Even if you do not care about the contest, your card is being seen and read by someone who manages the bowl of cards. Business cards can also be left on counter tops and bulletin boards if you do not have a brochure or flyer handy.

Business cards can be printed with a template on any computer. Special business card stock is available at office supply stores and some grocery stores. If you do not want to design your own, a local printer can design and print one for you. Online printing companies let you design your card, but they print them on premium paper for a very low cost; sometimes you only have to pay for the shipping if you allow their name to be placed on the back.

Following are important things to keep on hand for your media kit.

Flyers

Use your benefit statement that you created earlier and create a flyer. The flyer can be the front of one sheet of paper with an elaborate or basic design. List your basic services, hours, and contact information. A picture of the center or a logo is appropriate if space allows. A flyer may be used to promote a specific activity, like a grand opening or an anniversary celebration.

Brochures

Think about creating a brochure to further explain your services. A brochure is a double-sided sheet of paper, folded or tri-folded, that goes into detail about all the services you offer. It can be done by a professional or designed by you on the computer. (See the resource guide for places to design your written documents). If you want a tri-fold design, a professional designer or printer may be the best bet so that the folds and margins line up properly. The only thing worse than not having a media kit is having parts of it look sloppy and unprofessional.

A brochure can be placed in the media kit or it can be placed at local businesses for their clients to pick up. It is yet another tool to get your services recognized and to draw families in.

Always carry business cards, brochures, and flyers with you. You never know when you will run in to a person who may be looking for child care services. If you strike up a conversation, you can always hand them a card or flyer with the information so you know they have it instead of just relying on their memory. And when you are out and about, stick a brochure or two on the community billboard in the post office. Leave some business cards on the counter at the video store (make sure to get approval before dropping them). Anywhere you go is a potential place to advertise. Many stores, especially in smaller towns, rely on bulletin boards in the grocery store, post office, bank, and hardware stores to promote local activities and businesses.

NON-TRADITIONAL ADVERTISING

Non-traditional print advertising is a fun way to promote your business. Many of these methods are free or have little cost, except for your time and effort.

Bookmarks

If there is a library close by, create a bookmark with your logo and contact information that can be handed out to their patrons. Leave a stack in their resource rack. Ask to leave a stack on the desk or near the computer section.

Miscellaneous Merchandise

Office items can be a practical and fun way to get your name out. Pencils can be printed with a name and phone number relatively inexpensively by mail order and a specialty printer. Pens can also be printed with your contact information, but they cost a little bit more than pencils do. Stationary with your logo on the top or bottom is a great way to take notes. Other office items that can be imprinted are folders, binders, magnets, calendars, and letter openers. They can be handed out as random prizes to your families and employees or as prizes for the various contests you sponsor.

Sponsorships

Sponsor a coloring contest in the local newspaper. Put in a picture of your center (black and white and open for coloring, of course) in the paper and make up several categories for winners. Offer prizes to the winners. Advertise that all of the entries will be on display in your building and everyone can come in and look around. Even if you can only offer small prizes, offer something. Donate goods with your logo and business name. Pencils, t-shirts for the kids, and ball caps spread the word around just as well as standard print advertising.

Halloween

Along with your treat, include a flyer in children's goody bags. Make it a business card or bookmark attached to a candy bar. Affix a label with your information to the side of a bag of fruit snacks.

CREATE A BUZZ

When there does not seem to be much buzz going on, create it. Schedule some new advertising, schedule activities to generate interest, or find an alternative way to get the buzz going.

Press Releases

A press release can be a great link to the media. Press releases can be faxed or e-mailed to radio stations, TV channels, and magazines. When you are sending a press release, certain elements are needed to gain the interest of those receiving it. For instance, a press release should state who you are: Are you a private individual, a corporation, a small business, or a large business? How long have you been in business? What is your specialty?

Second, you need to include what it is you are sending the press release about. Are you having a grand opening celebration? An anniversary blow out party? A limited time only, reduced membership fee recruiting session? Why are you having this promotion, celebration, or party?

Third, include a specific date if you are putting on an event. If it is a newsworthy item, simply say what has happened in what month or during the last two months, this has been happening.

Last, include a contact person for people to call if they want further information or have questions. If the press release will be turned in to a newspaper article, they will include your name (or the name listed on the press release) to call for details. When this happens, prepare to be by the phone. Have a sheet handy with any or all of the activity details so you can quickly and efficiently answer questions.

A press release is typically one page in length. It has a few paragraphs detailing your news item or event and then the contact information. They are short and sweet and not too difficult to write. When time is short or you do not want to learn how to write one, you can also contact a freelance writer to construct one for you. For a separate fee, some writers even handle the distribution of the press release to various news agencies.

See the resource section for an example of a written press release and where to contact freelance writers for hire.

Activities

Other forms of marketing and advertising include newsworthy coverage. Is your child care center participating in an Arbor Day activity? Create a press release about what you are doing and send it to all of the news networks, TV, and radio. One of them may do a short write up or a blurb, but they may also send a reporter with a camera if they are intrigued. A reporter may take pictures of the children, interview you, or a child. Make it known you are doing this as a center activity and why – you want the children to learn about the environment, care about their town, etc.

Anniversary

Actively celebrate your anniversary every year. Plan an event with the children during the day. Have some games, fill some balloons, and serve cake. Take pictures to include in your scrapbook or future marketing materials. The anniversary celebration can be turned in to an open house style event for families and the neighborhood. Open your doors for the whole community to visit. Display pictures of all your year round activities. Treat it like a festival and offer prizes and refreshments all evening long.

Field Trips

Give your field trips extra meaning. Take an outing to the local nursing home during the holidays and sing Christmas carols. The residents love to see the smiling faces of children and enjoy hearing them sing. Send a press release announcing your plans so they can get pictures for an article or news clip. Visiting nursing homes is more than just a field trip; it is a service that you can provide to the elderly, who are often lonely during the year and especially the holidays.

A trip to a nature center may also be a service to the community. Is there an event planned for Earth Day? Can the children help clean a favorite hiking path after a long winter? Is there a place that needs raking or weed picking? These are great ways for the children to interact with nature, provide a community service, and have fun at the same time. Send a press release so the media can catch your children having fun and serving their community.

Community Marketing

You created an awesome media kit, but you do not know where or how to use it effectively. It is a shame to let it go to waste, so here are some great ways to send out media bits. You may have never even thought about these places as a way to advertise. They may even get better results for you than paid advertising.

Newcomer Clubs

With the transient nature of the young generation, newcomer clubs are becoming more popular in suburban and metro areas. Check the phone book or online and see if there is one for your city, your county, or your region. Some areas will have several distinctions for newcomers. The newcomers may also join more than one group, so investigate all of them. Get in touch with their leader and see if they have a packet of information that they give to all new residents of the area. If they do, ask to include your brochure or business card in the materials handed out. When they do accept your literature, ask about how many new member folders they give out each week or month and give them an adequate number of copies for that time frame. Check back periodically and give them an ample supply to fill more folders as they need to. Remember that the spring and summer are the busiest seasons for moving, so having extra to give to them during that time would be beneficial.

If the newcomer club does not provide a folder of local and regional information, take the bull by the horns and offer to do it. This would be a great sponsorship project. Use a folder with a label of your company information on the bottom to hold all the other information sheets and brochures you get from your area. You can actually assemble the folders or you can provide the folders and have the club do the gathering and assembling of the materials. It all depends on how well they are funded and staffed and how active they are in your area.

Chamber of Commerce

Becoming a member of the Chamber of Commerce can boost your business image. Becoming a member shows you care about your business and other businesses in town and want to work together to promote each other. The Chamber usually produces a list of members each year in a catalog or brochure, and details their business and contact information. While there is usually a membership fee for joining the Chamber of Commerce, the catalog mailings, and advertising therein are all free. Referrals from other Chamber businesses are also free, and could be more valuable than paid advertising.

Doctors and Dentists

Who patronizes doctor and dentist offices at least half of the time? Families with children. While mom is sitting in the waiting room, she could be looking over a brochure that is sitting on the counter. Or she could have picked up your business card or flyer that was posted on the bulletin board. Doctors and dentists have a large number of clients from a wide ranging area, and you should reach out to them. Ask permission from the receptionist, doctor, or dentist to see if they would be willing to place your information or give it out. If they are willing to let you post on a bulletin board, check back often to see that your flyer is not vandalized or torn. When it does get worn, replace it with a fresh copy so it always looks professional. Check on your brochure stack and refill them if they are getting low.

Moving Companies

Not everyone who moves in to a new region joins a newcomer club. But you will still want to reach them. One way to do so is with a moving company. Treat the moving company the same way you would a newcomer club. Ask if they have a packet of information they hand out to their clients and if you can be included in it. If they do not, again offer to sponsor a packet by providing folders (complete with logo, business card, and brochure).

Certain moving companies are more inclusive and offer a lot of services in addition to moving for their clients. They may represent corporate transfers or a relocation service independent of large companies. And there are always companies who move from state to state and county to county for individuals. Explore every one of them.

Realtors

You have already hit upon the newcomer club for people who are new to the area and moving companies for those who may not join a newcomer club, so that is everybody, right? Nope. Families and individuals with children move within town, across town, or to the next county. They do not need moving services because they have family that can help. They have lived in the area for several years and do not want to join a newcomer group. So, the next thing – hit the realtors.

Realtors often provide services to their clients who are buying homes. A folder is made up of all the local doctors, dentists, veterinarian offices, schools, parks, and child care centers. Make sure to get your name on the list. If possible, give them a stack of brochures to include in the packet of information or to keep at their office if people ask about local services. Check back frequently and replenish their supply if needed.

OB/GYN Offices

These doctors get special mention. Other doctors may not have as many children or families in their care, but you know an OB is all about children. And families who are seeking the care of an OB are already planning a family, and every single one of them is a potential client for you.

If you are limited on time or money in the brochure copies and placement, opt for OB offices before family practices or pediatricians. Families and individuals with older children may already have care in place, but someone with a new baby may have not made arrangements yet. They can be a prime market.

Create a specialty flyer for OB offices that details the care you provide to infants and toddlers. It is important to include all your business information, as they may have older siblings, but focus on what care you could provide that new baby they are expecting. Have your contact information present on the flyer, but not what your rates are. You want interested families to call so you can get a feel for them and what services they are looking for before they decide they want to go with you.

Always Be on the Lookout

You never know when an opportunity will arise, and you can promote your business. During your weekly rituals, such as taking your children to swimming class, making a deposit at the bank, or picking up a book of stamps, look around. Are there bulletin boards in the entryway full of other local businesses? Is there a place to display business cards? Do they have a counter full of brochures and flyers for local events? To make sure you are always prepared, carry business cards with you at all times: a handful in your purse, a stack in the glove compartment box, or a pack in the swimming bag. You can at least stick a business card up and return with flyers or brochures at a later date since you know they have a place to hang them. Make sure it is free or approved before you post your information. Most places do not have a charge, but it is best to check first. And other places require approval (with signatures or initials) of your materials before they can be hung up for public viewing.

Get Online

With millions of people surfing the Internet everyday, you may want to incorporate the Internet into your marketing and advertising campaign. Using the Internet can be as simple as posting a listing in the yellow pages online section. Or it can be as complex as having an interactive, flash Web site for your business.

The beauty of having a Web site is that it can be a tool to market to both potential and current families. When marketing to potential clients, you can have pictures of every room, pictures and profiles of all your staff, program information, sample daily schedules, the current newsletter in downloadable form, and the current food menu. A Web site can also give specials like a coupon for the month of June to get free diaper service or pay for one summer camp for school-aged children, get the second one 25 percent off. Coupons and running promotions online will not cost extra like running a newspaper or radio ad does.

Marketing to current families can include online, up to the minute, updated account information. Parents can check out their child's daily activities by viewing pictures, weekly lesson plans, teacher updates, and anything else you can imagine. Progress reports can be made accessible with passwords, as well as daily activity sheets. The only thing that limits what is on your Web site is your time and your budget for the creation of the space.

The convenience of Web sites is what may earn you business. If a mother is too busy during her workday to call, she can get just as much information from your site at 1 a.m. as she could with a phone call during business hours. The same convenience holds true for current families. A dad wants to check on the weekly progress of his three-year-old, but it was too hectic at pick up time to ask you or the teacher. So he logs in, goes to the separate page for his child's room, looks at all of last week's pictures, reads what they are learning this week, and access his child's progress report, all at midnight. Having a Web site might actually be a time saver for you, too.

How to Get Hooked Up

You love the Internet and are online all the time, but you do not know how to create your own Web site. Nor do you want to take the time and learn. There are several ways you can find people to create awesome Web sites for you.

Before you hire someone to build a Web site, you need to devise a budget. How much upfront money can you invest in the initial design? A standard, informational page with a few links and graphics can cost as little as a couple hundred dollars. An elaborate site, with forums, message boards, profile registration for families, and account accessibility will be much more expensive.

Any type of Web site will have a monthly fee from whichever server or domain name is your host. Depending upon how much bandwidth you use, the cost can range from $4.95 per month to $99.95 per month. Bandwidth is determined by how much space you are taking up on the host's networks. Straight text takes up little room, but pictures, graphics, and multiple pages use up quite a bit more.

Once you settle on a budget, you need to find your creator. The first place to search is your local Chamber of Commerce directory. See if there is a Web site developer in your area. If so, and they also belong to the Chamber, you may get a discount in services. The next place to search would be in the phone book under Web site designers, graphic designers, and maybe even Web domain hosting. All these places will have Internet savvy people, and if they cannot do what you need them to, chances are they know someone who can and will refer you to them.

Your search can then take you online to freelance Web sites. These sites allow you to post your project and enables providers to bid on the projects. This is a good way to have work done because the providers give fair and accurate bids since they are competing on your work, and you can view past references from previous projects, you can see a portfolio of samples and links, and you can ask questions of each potential provider before you award a project. See the resource section for a list of freelance designer's Web sites.

WHAT TO DO AFTER YOU GET THE WORD OUT

You have spent tons of time getting the word out about your business, so now what do you do? Be prepared to answer any and all questions about yourself and your business anytime, anywhere.

Prospective phone calls will come in at any time on any day, so you need to be prepared. If you are not the only person who will be answering the phones, makes sure every other person is trained in dealing with prospective families. You need to answer the phone in a friendly manner and address the needs of the caller. If they are seeking your services, get some information out of them. Ask questions to get a feel for their needs. Get their contact information for future calls or place them on your waiting list if you are full. Make notes so you can remember if they call again or come in for an interview.

Keep information sheets by the phone at all times. For example, if there is a special promotion going on that month; if you have an activity scheduled during the month where the public is invited; if you have any change in plans, policy, or details, have it documented by the phone. That way, when whomever answers the phone and gets the question, "What time does your festival start on Saturday?" they have the information right away. There is no fumbling around, asking who has the information and playing phone tag to deliver the correct information or lost messages.

The worst thing you can do for your business is to spend hundreds of dollars on advertising or many hours of sweat and toil on a project or activity and then let the ball drop. Sharp advertising and great news feature stories can be forgotten in an instant if a return call is not placed or incorrect follow up information is given out. When other people are in your employ and answer the phone, give them some training as to what to say. A heads up at the beginning of the week to let them know you have an ad with a coupon coming out or you have begun a recruiting campaign is necessary so you are all on the same page.

Schedule an Interview

If you have an opening, schedule a family interview. This is where they can ask any and all questions about your services, and you can also get a feel for them. Give them all the answers they need to make an informed decision about the care of their child. This is a very important step for you and the parents to determine if it will be a good match. If the children are along, observe them and their behavior. Discuss any special needs they may have.

Things to consider discussing in your parent interview:

- How many children?

- What are the ages of the children?

- What hours will they need care?

- Any allergies? Special needs?

- Describe your child and their interests.

- How did they hear about you?

Give a Tour

If the interview portion goes well and the family appears interested, offer a tour of your home or facility. Explain where the sleeping areas are and how you go about meal preparation. Give them a tour of the outside play areas as well as the inside play areas.

If you are a large child care center provider, show them the specific rooms where the child(ren) will be. Introduce them to the provider(s) in the room and let them look around. Have their children interact with the children in the other room.

You do not want to give a hard sell to any potential families, but you want to make it clear you provide a safe and caring child care environment for all the children involved.

Upon their leaving, offer them a registration packet if you think they are serious about using your services. If they were just browsing, you will be able to tell by the amount and type of questions they ask. For instance, if they only asked what the weekly fee was and then lost interest, chances are they will not be returning. If a parent asks repeated questions about the schedule, the staff, the policies, and the fees, they are probably more interested and will return.

Keep a contact sheet for every family you interview. Make notes about what questions they asked, how the tour went, and what your impression was. The family may not call back right away. If they call several months down the road, you should be able to pull out their information sheet and refresh your memory quickly. They may also be impressed with your memory and organization skills if you remember their name.

Another thing to keep track of on their info sheet is any concerns that you have about them or their child. Was the child angry? Rude? Misbehaving? And the same notes can be taken for the parents. Did they ignore their child? Did they say anything that put up a red flag with you as far as payment issues? Hours?

Refusing Care

There will come a time when you will need to refuse service to a family. When this occurs, make sure you are not refusing on the basis of discrimination. You do have legal rights to refuse a family based on information you have received or are given.

One reason to refuse care for a family is if they refuse to give you the name of their previous child care provider. This may be simply because they do not want you to have contact with them. However, it could also mean that they were not good clients. They may have been delinquent payers, the child may have had serious behavior issues, or the family simply failed to follow the sick child policy. Either way, their repeated refusal should indicate there is a reason they are looking for new child care service.

Another reason to refuse service is the behavior of the child. If you observe that the child is out of control, there may be serious issues that you are not being told about. The issues may not only be behavioral, they could stem from a situation at home that is not positive. While you want what is best for the child, you also need to consider what is best for the children already entrusted in your care.

Sometimes a family will want certain services that you just cannot provide within your means. If they have a child with a severe food allergy, but are not willing to help out in supplying the specialty foods they need, you are not responsible for picking up the extra tab. Some allergies require children to bypass milk and have all soy products. Soy is more expensive and will cost more to provide. And if they cannot have dairy products, you will have to alter the rest of your meals to accommodate them.

Lack of respect by the parents may result in a denial of service. If a parent does not seem interested in you or the provider in the room their child will be in, it may signal a larger problem. If they do not care about what is going on in the day to day setting, if they ignore or disregard communication by the provider, or if they flat out refuse to compromise on something, you are entitled to excuse that family.

Last, a reason to not take on a family is if they outright disagree with your payment policy. Chances are that if they balk before even using your services, they will have a hard time paying you on time or at all. If they cannot pay or do not agree to your services, they should look elsewhere for the care of their child.

If a family is already enrolled in your program, there are other reasons you will have to terminate their contract and end care for their children. See Chapter 12 for details.

MARKETING TO CURRENT CLIENTS

Not only will you need to market to potential families you will care for, but you need to continue marketing to the families who are already in your care. The marketing will not be to get their business, but to keep their business and have them refer friends. Following are ways to market to families already in your care.

Bulletin Board

Hang a bulletin board by the door or prominent place where parents walk by on a daily or weekly basis. This will be a great place to hang announcements, center news, upcoming events, policy changes, illness updates, and activities. Make a place where parents can hang up notes, too – carpooling information, where can I find, who can I call. Monitor any information that is hung on the board to make sure it is relevant and family oriented. Keep the information current; remove old news and activity sheets that have expired. A bulletin board full of old, useless information is almost the same as not even having one.

Newsletter

Create a monthly newsletter. Explain to the families what will be going on during the upcoming month. Will you be having any field trips, what parties will be going on, are there any days when you will be closed or need a few hours to go to a doctor's appointment? What will your education program be focusing on this month? Is there any training you or your staff members will be having this month? Share it; let your families know how much time and commitment it takes to be a well-trained care giver.

You can also do a lot of fun things with a newsletter. Share children's birthdays, family anniversary dates, student or family of the week, promotions, etc. Use some fun clip art or have the children draw pictures and include them in the monthly exhibit. Whatever it is, make it fun.

Greeting Cards

Take a minute and acknowledge your families. Send cards in the mail for birthdays or major holidays, like Christmas. Taking the time to send a personal greeting or remembering their special day will let them know you care about them and their business. A thoughtful caregiver will keep their current families happy, and when current families are happy and satisfied, they provide great word of mouth exposure. Word of mouth is the best type of advertising and publicity you could ask for.

Monthly Promotions

Create a reason to have a monthly promotion. The family who brings in the most Box Tops for Education for February will receive a T-shirt (with your logo of course) for everyone in the family. The family who refers the most new clients for a month gets 10 percent off their next month's tuition. Add some hype – give a great reward and you will get a positive response. Anything with hype and a prize, no matter how small, can seem like a great "contest." They might not even see that you are actively recruiting names of new families.

Referrals

Always show your current clients that you care about their support. Whenever you receive a referral, have a prize set up to reward them, no matter if it is a monthly promotion or not. For instance, each time a family is sent to you by a current or former family in your care, send them a gift certificate to the ice cream store. Or offer a $5 or $10 rebate for each new family who signs up and joins your center. It does not have to be a large prize or even worth money, but it should be a token of your appreciation. Their referrals are of no cost to you and even more special, since they have taken the time to give your name and information out.

Yearly Contract Information

In addition to a monthly newsletter, you should think about having a year in review or a preview of the upcoming year. A year in review can discuss all the center improvements you have facilitated, new programs you or your teachers have been using with the children, new employees, training for any and all employees during the year, and the places you have visited on field trips or center outings. Month to month newsletters are great for the short term, but a year in review can paint the big picture for families and show just how important you consider their child's development.

A preview of the upcoming year can highlight any changes that will be taking place in your center. Will you be putting an addition on to your house? Is your center remodeling to accommodate more children? Do you plan to hire more employees to handle the care for more children? What activities do you hope to enjoy with the children? A year in preview can also bring up serious topics, such as a contract change or payment increase. While the new changes may not be going into effect immediately, this could be a way to ease the parents into paying a higher fee down the road. If they have ample forewarning, they are less likely to fuss over it. A preview can also discuss any new policy changes you will be enforcing, such as potty changing, education discipline, etc.

Evaluations

Evaluations are a great way to get feedback on your center, your employees, and your programs. The information can be returned anonymously, allowing more families to complete the information honestly, if they are experiencing some difficulties.

The evaluations can be given on the family's year anniversary or you can give everyone an evaluation at the time of your center's anniversary. Ask what they are satisfied with in your center. What do they like? What things do their children like? You also want to know where you can improve. Are there services they would like to see offered? Do they have any concerns with staff members?

Take all the feedback and keep track of it. Write down any areas of concern and see how you can improve upon them. Do they feel you need more staffing? Think about hiring more. Do they want to see more outdoor playtime? Schedule more. If they have reasonable cause for concern, address it. Is there a staff member who has a harder time getting along with the children than others? Maybe they need more training or classes on dealing with young children. If that does not work, you may have to think further down the road and consider letting this person go.

NEGATIVE MEDIA

While it should not happen very often, negative or wrongful media coverage will occur. Whether it is about you, your child care center, or an event that happened on the national level, you need to be prepared as to how to best deal with it.

An event happens across the state or across the country where a child care provider has an error in judgment. An illness, an injury, or even a death could have resulted. What you need to do is reassure your clients that this will not happen in your home or center. Copy news articles so that they know that it did happen. Counter that information with a copy of your policy, whether it is the sickness policy, the medicine policy, or the discipline policy. Restate your policy to them in person, and assure them that this is a rare case.

When it is an event that occurred in your home or your center, be honest. You may want to consider sending a letter and detailing the incident or as much as you can, so they understand what happened and why. It will be easiest for a large center to send a letter since speaking individually to all the parents may take several days. A note in each child's mailbox can inform the parent, and if they want more specifics or a meeting with you, they can schedule it at a more convenient time.

An event can happen that may require terminating an employee. If it is an incident that several children or parents know about, you may want to disclose it to everyone before the news were to get out via another method. Nothing is worse for a parent than finding out second hand or from the TV that something happened at their child care center. Reassure all your families that the employee was relieved, and you are taking measures to educate and train any and all future staff to prevent this incident from happening again.

Sometimes a report to the media can even be wrong. A disgruntled employee or terminated family may report an event that is taken out of context or simply did not happen. If this occurs, document exactly what is said. If the accusations are way off base or completely unfounded, you may have grounds for a libel or slander case. Make sure to inform your families of what is going on and to refute the untrue statements so they are reassured and will remain in your care. An untrue statement can cause you to lose business or even future business, so handle the situation with extreme care. If the public relations end up messy, you may want to hire a professional consultant in order to deal with it quickly and effectively.

"A little girl is sugar and spice and everything nice

- especially when she's taking a nap."

~Author Unknown

8
GOALS & OBJECTIVES

A business is like a ship. If it has no heading, it does not know in which direction to travel. Like any good trip, the route must be planned carefully. The same is true with your business. You cannot arrive at a destination without directions.

Setting your business off in the right direction requires planning. You need to know where you want to go in order to get anywhere. One way to do so is by creating goals and objectives. These goals do not only have to be financial goals. You can create a set of goals and objectives for your employees, your enrollment numbers, your financial status, and your educational programs.

GOALS

When you set your goals, you want to make them attainable and realistic. Nothing is more frustrating than a goal that is so far-fetched, you know you can never reach it.

A sample goal for your business may be to increase the number of children in attendance. At the beginning of the last school year you had 23 full-time children and another 12 who attended the after school program. This year, you would like to increase your full-time children to at least 25 and your after school program to at least 15 children.

In order to meet these goals, you will need adequate time to prepare. You will need to advertise in some fashion, via print or word of mouth. One of the best ways to get more children in the after school program is to enlist the help of the students currently in it. Ask them if they have any friends or know of someone in their class that needs child care after school. If they do, and you know they are responsible enough, send a brochure or a flyer with them to school. If the after school children are happy with your program, they will often recruit other friends to join them anyway. Children like to have their friends around, even if they see each other all day long.

Another way to enlist more students is to advertise in a newspaper or circular focusing on family issues. Place a coupon or special that gives them an added incentive to enlist your services. Give them half off their first month's fee or waive the registration costs. Both are low cost to you, but they do not need to know that. They see that they are getting something for free, in addition to a great service.

Mission Statement

The first order of business will be to create a mission statement. The mission statement should encompass your goals, your services, and your high quality of standards in performing each. Make sure to print several copies, frame them, and hang them around the building so your employees can see it, read it, believe it, and most of all, follow it. Even a home child care provider needs to have a mission statement printed out, framed, and hung up. A mission statement tells your employees and the families in your care what you are about.

What Do You Want to Achieve?

You also need to plan what you want to achieve through the different services you offer. Do you want the highest profit margin from services you offer? Do you want to make your families' lives easier by offering convenience services? Do you want to offer a valuable service for families in need of services in your area? The services you should offer depend on your goals. If you want to make the largest profit possible, offer all the services with fees passed on to the families. If you have a community that is economically sluggish, but child care is still required, you may offer low cost care or government assisted care. When factories or companies run three shifts of workers, alternative hours will be popular.

No matter which of these services you provide, you need to set a clear goal for it. For example, you are willing to open your doors for second and third shift workers; however, you need to maintain six children during each shift for it to remain feasible to do so. When you are successful at keeping those numbers, think about raising the number and expanding your program after a few years. Make the number realistic and attainable so you are not setting yourself up for failure. Have a plan of action so you know what to do when and if the numbers were to stay below six children on one shift. Do you actively recruit more? Do you withhold services for the other five? Do you overcompensate in other areas?

Financial goals can be tricky to plan. When you are a startup business, you will operate in the red for a while until you can recoup some of the initial expenses. Your financial goals are more realistic to set annually. That way, if you have a slow month, and others are good, they will balance out overall.

Financial goals are not only related to your revenue, but also to your spending. Keep budgets set and monitor their success. If one budget keeps missing, it may need to be reevaluated so your overall goals can be met the following year.

Besides budgets and expenses, the economy in your region can play a role in your success. Economic slumps can affect your success whether you like it or not. A corporation goes under, a recession causes widespread lay offs, or a buyout moves a business location. If the parents do not have work, they will not have need for your services. Planning for economic slides is hard. Going in to business is always a gamble, but it can be less risky with a little planning. When a backup plan is in place, the stress of having financial difficulties is not as stressful (or less so if you know there is money in place to pay the bills).

Part 3

Open For

Business

You have already had, or will soon be having, your grand opening. Now what? It is time to settle in and make your business profitable and successful. To achieve success financially and academically, you need to set and follow many different business policies. Even if you have a small in home child care center, you will need to have a path to follow to achieve the maximum benefits for everyone involved.

9
BUSINESS POLICIES

Running a day care center, whether it is in your home or another building, is not all fun and child's play. You will need to set up policies, follow them strictly, and make sure any and all employees do, too, to remain successful.

Admission Policies

The first consideration is what type of children you can accept. There are families with child care needs for children who have disabilities. Those disabilities may range from mild to severe. They may be physical or mental. Some of them may include, but are not limited to, ADD, ADHD, epilepsy, autism, asthma, PKU, food allergies, diabetes, cystic fibrosis, and hearing problems. You cannot discriminate against someone with a handicap, whether it is physical or mental. However, you have the right to not provide care if their situation requires more resources than what you can provide.

Many children with a physical disability need special facilities. Do you have ramps for wheelchairs or walkers? Are your doorknobs accessible for everyone? Those are just the tip of the iceberg. Each individual with a physical disability will need to be evaluated on their own to make a determination of their specific needs. According to the ADA (Americans with Disabilities Act) if they have reasonable needs, you need to make the effort to provide them. You can only turn them away if they need more equipment than you can reasonably buy and maintain.

Physically and mentally disabled children usually need extra attention. Whether you work alone or with a staff, you only have so many helping hands. When considering a child with a disability, you need to take into account how much attention they will require. Do they need one on one support all the time? Do they require special attention, but not constant? The ADA also recognizes this as being true, but again, you cannot discriminate unless they are truly beyond your means. If they need constant attention, their rate may be much higher since they will affect your staffing.

Many families cannot afford the full rate of child care costs. The government has a program set up where they pay a percentage of the childcare costs that the family cannot afford. Each state is different, but many require special approval and certifications in order to qualify as being a state endorsed provider. If you are approved, the family pays you what they can and you must fill out paperwork and apply to the state to be reimbursed for the rest.

The downfall of watching government-assisted families is that you are putting forth the work before being paid and run the risk of being burned if the family quits before the government paperwork is processed. A check from the government will be mailed directly to you, after a period of about six weeks.

The positives of providing for subsidized families are that once you are approved, you are always approved. And there is always a need for daycare with these families, so there may be no shortage of children needing quality care.

There are a few reasons why you would deny a family admission to your child care center. You do not and cannot provide adequate building facilities for them, you cannot provide one on one staff for what they are willing to pay, or you would need too much specialized food for their diet in order for them to attend your center.

Other tricky reasons to deny admission to your home or center is if you know or strongly suspect that their will be a personality clash. You cannot discriminate for any reason against a family or child, but if you believe their will be problems, you have just reason to deny their care. If you provide it in writing, they should have no recourse to sue you for discrimination later.

FEES

Once you decide who you will accept, you need to determine how much you will charge for services. Not only will you have to determine your weekly fee for the child, you will have extra fees to consider. Do you instill fees for children who are being potty trained? Do you offer an early morning opening for a fee? What are your late payment charges? Late pickup fees?

Fees for child care expenses can be as varied as you (or your accountant) want to deal with or as basic as one flat fee. You may also want to take into account what the going rate is in your area.

For full-time care, consider what services you provide. Do you provide meals and snacks or do they bring their own? Do you provide diapers and wipes or do they? Factor all of your expenses like staffing, materials, and supplies in to a weekly rate per child. Giving discounts to multiple children per family will also be at your discretion. See Chapter 8 for a more in-depth discussion of determining your rate.

If you have several children who attend part-time or want to find part-time or after school only children, you may think of an hourly or part time rate. Hourly rates can be confusing and hard to keep track of in a large center, but are easily managed in a home child care setting. Part-time rates will also attract those working families in which one parent works two or three days outside of the home.

Other fees that you might want to instill are fees for late pickup. If a parent has not picked up a child after your closing time, a per minute or five minute rate is acceptable. It will certainly cut down on the amount of times people are late. Charging for your overtime will also cut down on families trying to take advantage of you.

If you have a lot of paperwork to fill out for each child, whether it is for the state or yourself, an enrollment fee is also an option. The enrollment fee is usually nominal and covers the amount of time you spend copying, filling out, and filing the necessary paperwork.

It is also a good policy to set up late payment fees. Sometimes things get tough, but it is not an excuse to withhold payment. When payment is not received on the due date, add an extra fee on top if it is not received by the next day or within the following five days. Repeat offenders may also require an additional fee if they consistently miss payments. Excessive missed payments may be cause for termination of your service agreement.

Even though the children you care for may feel like family, you need to prepare yourself for their departures. It is a courtesy for a family to give you two weeks notice if they will not be in need of your services any longer. If they do not give you two weeks notice, require them to pay a two-week fee regardless if they use your services for those two weeks.

HOURS OF OPERATION

Now that you know how much you will charge each family, you need to determine your hours. If you are a single person in a home center, it would be hard to manage open hours of 6 a.m. to 6 p.m. However, if you were a large center, you could run several shifts and cover it easily. You will need to determine a schedule that can be slightly flexible, but cover the needs of most working people.

Set up what holidays you will be closed and put it in writing. Send a calendar with your closed dates out at the beginning of the year for every family. When the dates get close, hang a sign or remind the families that you will be closed and they need to make other arrangements. Also, note whether you are to be paid for these days or if they get a discounted rate for the week.

SERVICES

The services which you provide may not be an actual service, but they are a benefit to the families in your care. Large daycare centers have more flexibility in offering services to their families. Typically, the more people who use the service makes the fee go down. With home centers having a small number of families, the fees may be too high to make certain services an option. Either way, it is up to each individual to decide what services you want to offer.

Below are some of the services you can offer as a provider or large child care center.

FOOD SERVICE

Food service means that you or your center will be providing all of the food needed for a child every day. Food services can be minimal or catered to your center's needs. If you are open early or late, offering a breakfast or dinner program may be a smart option. These meals are not "normal" daily fare, so an optional fee would be required to cover the costs.

The Pros of Offering Food Service

- Food services can usually be subsidized by the government food program if they meet certain standards. Therefore, if you follow their regulations, like serve a fruit and vegetable at lunch and a healthy snack in the afternoon, you will be reimbursed a percentage by the state.

- You know how many children will be eating every day and can plan the food purchases accordingly. You also will not have to worry about who forgot their lunch or snack and have to make up for it.

The Cons of Offering Food Service

- There is more paperwork involved. You will need to plan menus and mail them in for approval each month.

- You will need to follow a set of rules for cooking and what foods are allowed to be served. The rules are not stringent, but it is another set of rules to be complied with.

- There will be one meal per time; therefore, some children will eat it and some will not. You cannot cater to individual taste buds, so some children may go hungry on certain days of the week.

AFTER SCHOOL CARE PROGRAMS

There is a big gap between the number of providers who take after school only children compared to the need for them. No matter if it is a large center or a small one, they often will not take a child who only needs before or after school time hours. At most, a school-aged child would have an hour or two before school and another hour or two after. Since parents work different shifts or can stagger their work times, usually only one of the times is needed.

The Pros of Before/After School Care

- If you keep children before or after school or both, you will have more steady, albeit a smaller income. If you have a bigger center, the times of when children arrive and depart may be far enough apart that you can juggle your staff to accommodate the change.

The Cons of Before/After School Care

- In home and smaller centers only have a limited number of children they are licensed for. The limited hours earn less revenue than if they could hold that spot for a full-time paying child. However, with families who have multiple children, it is not always an option to say no to an after school child. Saying no may force the family to go elsewhere so that all of their children can be cared for in one location. If they leave, you are left with less income than if you had kept the part-time child.

SUMMER CAMPS

Summer camps are for children who attend school full-time during the year. They are not old enough to stay home alone during the summer days, but too old to sit in a child care setting. Summer camps can be themed around any number of activities like sports, hobbies, themes, or arts and crafts.

The Pros of Offering Summer Camps

- The convenience of keeping all the children in a one-day care setting for families is wonderful. If they do not have to run around, drop off, and pick up three different children to three different centers, they will probably even pay extra. The relief of having care that is familiar to them may also make them be loyal and a great word of mouth referral.

- Since it is summer time, there are many college students who are looking for part-time work. Finding additional staff may be easy in the summer months. It may even prove to be easier than during the other times of the year, when you need full-time staff.

- Planning a summer camp theme may be fun. It gives you a chance to step outside your normal routine and plan something different. If you are the one working with the older kids, you may actually get to be outside more and enjoy the summer days.

- Offering a summer camp is a great way to earn some additional revenue. The additional older children will need less staff overall; therefore, they could have higher profit return percentages.

The Cons of Offering Summer Camps

- Bigger children will need bigger spaces. You need a large enough area to hold all these bigger children in all kinds of weather conditions. You can plan on them playing in the park the majority of the time, but only in good weather. When a blistering heat wave happens or a torrential rainfall is expected the children will need somewhere indoors to stay.

- With having additional children in your care, you will need additional supplies. Additional supplies include food, paper products, forms, and equipment. And older children tend to use more, eat more, and play more than younger children do, so they may go through supplies extra fast.

- Another consideration for having extra children is the extra staff you will need. Older children have a much higher ratio of adults to children, but you still need to pay for staffing. One staff person may not be enough since you do not want to send a lone adult on a field trip or adventure.

NON-TRADITIONAL HOURS/AFTER HOURS CARE

The demand for non-traditional hours in child care is growing. Many households are run by single parents who work an afternoon or night shift and need care for their children. Sometimes both parents in a household work an afternoon or night shift job. Relying on other family members is not always an option. Non-traditional hours for child care centers could mean being open for afternoon only hours, like three in the afternoon until midnight. Or they may choose to only be open for nighttime hours and open at nine and close at six or seven in the morning. Many centers will offer non-traditional hours of service in additional to day hours, resulting in 24 hour care centers.

The Pros of Non-Traditional Care

- Non-traditional hours are desperately needed by some families and demand could be high. If you are in high demand, your prospects will never run low, and you will be able to maintain full capacity and generate high revenue.

- Another positive with being open during non-traditional hours is that you may be able to find staff that does not like to work non-traditional hours, too. Or it may be a great second or part-time job for young teachers or college students. Even though many people prefer day hours to work, there are many people that like to have a varied schedule.

The Cons of Non-Traditional Care

- If you are an in home provider, you will need to adjust your routine. If you have young children, they will need to alter their schedules to fit with your work schedule. It may only be a slight shift of your schedule, but it is a shift.

- Providing non-traditional hours care will also reduce the amount of alone time you have with your own kids. If your kids go to school, there will always be someone else around during the dinner and after dinner hours. If you normally do any extra curricular activities, like sports, boy scouts or girl scouts, or church activities, you will need to arrange for rides for your child or have adequate room to take everyone along.

• Even though there may be people who like to work alternative hours, finding qualified staff may be hard. Working an afternoon shift means giving up evening hours at home or with the family, which is hard for people to do.

DROP IN CARE

Drop in care means a person does not have a regular schedule every week, but needs care every week. They may work Monday, Tuesday, and Wednesday one week, but Thursday and Friday only the next week. Nurses, firefighters, and other medical professionals usually have rotating shifts where they need full-time care, but not on a daily basis.

The Pros of Drop in Care

• If you have enough drop in children, you may be able to balance the schedule and pick up more children if the schedules work out with your licensing numbers. If you can have more children at different times of the day without overlapping, your income will be higher.

The Cons of Drop in Care

• Keeping the schedule may prove difficult and confusing. If work schedules change with only a moment's notice, you will not be able to bounce around other families to make space. Being over your licensed limit with children is not an option, so you would have to turn someone away, which is also not a good option.

• If the drop in hours were very few each week, you would have a hard time getting to know the child or settling into a normal routine. If the child had a hard time settling in to a routine, they may act out or misbehave. And if the hours remain very low, the time involved may not be worth the amount of money.

PART-TIME CARE

Since many mothers are not working full-time outside of the home, there is a large demand for part-time care. As with drop in care and after or before school hours, the income potential with part timers could be small. Part-time would account for children who only need half days or two or three days per week.

The Pros of Part-Time Care

- If you get the right mixture of families, you can schedule your part-time children to balance schedules. You will get more money with more children, as long as their times do not overlap.

The Cons of Part-Time Care

- Juggling a schedule. As long as the schedules remain consistent, you could balance with another family. However, if someone needed to change or to become a drop in, you would not be able to care for him or her. If you are left with only a few part-time children, you might only have a part time income.

WEEKEND CARE

With more and more untraditional jobs in the marketplace, there are more untraditional hours needed for childcare. Certain professions work on weekends and only a few days during the week. They may need Saturday only in their standard work week or they may need Saturday and Sunday care for children.

The Pros of Weekend Care

- If you have children around the same age as your weekenders, your children will have playmates. And since there are very few providers who are open for weekend hours, you would probably never run out of families who needed your services.

The Cons of Weekend Care

- You would be essentially giving up your weekends, too. If you were only open for certain days during the week you could have a five-day work week and take days off to compensate, but chances are you do not. You will have other families that require Monday through Friday care, thus leaving you to work seven days a week.

- If you have your own children, you would be limiting what activities you could do with them. If you had other children, a spontaneous trip to the mall or the movie theater would probably be out of the question because of the expense involved. However, if the children you were watching were of similar age, their parents might offer the extra money to make up for it.

LAUNDRY SERVICE

Laundry service can range from cloth to only diapers. In theory, a large center would have a much greater need for laundry services than a home center would — or at least the cost would be justified more. A one-person operation could certainly use the help, but not usually afford the price tag.

The Pros of Offering Laundry Service

- Someone else does the dirty work while you focus on the kids or the business at hand. It takes one task off your to do list and frees up precious time for something else.

The Cons of Offering Laundry Service

- The expense. If you go with a cloth diaper service, there is a cost per child you will need to pass on to the families. The higher weekly rate might make them go somewhere else for child care services.

- The materials. If you use a laundry service for diapers and towels, chances are you will have to use what they supply. You will not get to pick your quality of diaper, towel, sheet, etc.

TRANSPORTATION SERVICE

Transportation can be a great service to provide. Whether you are picking up a group of after school children or shuttling to afternoon kindergarten, there are many things to take in to consideration.

The Pros of Transporting Children

- Your services will be more desirable. If you have the ability to drop a group of children off at boy scouts after school, you become that much more of a positive to a busy family. Even if a family has to pay extra for the service, they are willing to do so for the convenience.

The Cons of Transporting Children

- The liability. You are now not only responsible for the life of a child in the center, but you are responsible for them as they travel outside of the center. You will need to carry extra liability insurance to cover vehicles and any potential accidents that might occur.

- The expense. You will need to maintain any vehicle used for transporting children and have it meet safety standards with adequate seat belts and warning signs. If you are a home center, your regular vehicle will work. If you are a large center, you will need to purchase a passenger van.

- Scheduling. Once you commit to transporting children, you will have to be on time every time. You accept the responsibility of dropping them off or picking them up on time, even if schedules or other children try to interfere.

In short, the services you can offer any family who brings their children to you is mostly for convenience. Some of the convenience offered is for them, but some are for you. The more conveniences you offer, the more your services as a provider will appeal to families. The additional services like laundry and transportation should not be done just as a way to make a little more money. The services can make your business flow a little better and save you some precious time and energy in the process.

CONTRACTS

When the fees are determined and a family is accepted in to your care, you need a written contract. No matter how nice a family appears or how great their financial situation looks, you need to have proof in writing for your protection. And this protection is needed whether you care for three or 300 children.

A contract for care will spell out the terms you have settled on when agreeing to care for the child. The contract is a binding agreement stating you or your center will care for the child, what the weekly or monthly fee is, and when payments are due. This contract should be signed by both parties and possibly notarized or even approved by a legal representative.

To be even more thorough, you can create a contract packet to give to each family. A contract packet should include the fee, the payment due dates, any days your center will be closed, termination rules, and withdrawal policies.

This way, the family knows and signs that they agree to your rules.

The benefits of having a signed contract with each family are numerous.

Accountability

When a family wants you to care for their child and wants to pay for your services, they agree to pay you on time. They cannot try to change the amount later on or bend the rules to fit a special financial need. The contract states if there will be late fees and when. It states what penalties will be enforced when payment is not received after a specific amount of time.

Termination

With any other job, courtesy and professionalism dictate that you give two weeks notice to any employer. The same courtesy should be extended to any provider, whether it is a large centers or an in home child care center. When a family does not give you two weeks notice before removing the child, you still have the contract which will enforce that they need to pay you for two weeks, whether or not their child is in attendance.

Communication

A contract packet will give the family a list of all the dates you will be closed, either for holidays or vacation days if you operate from your house. If they know what days you are closed, they can make alternate arrangements ahead of time and be prepared. You do not want someone to show up at your house early because they forgot you were closed (even though you are at home on vacation) and beg to watch their child since they have nowhere else to go.

A written contract is legally binding, so if a family does become severely delinquent in payments, you have recourse to get your money. All fees, payments, and information needed by the family is listed in detail and their signature proves that they agreed.

10
BUSINESS PRACTICES

Your child care business is open and running. Now the challenge is to keep it running smoothly to maintain peak performance. While the focus of your business is on the care of the children, you will also need to have an office for your paperwork and financial matters.

The larger your center is, the more paperwork you will need to keep track of. Even in a home child care setting, it is very important to keep your personal receipts separate from your child care expenses. Receipts for supplies, wages, and food expenses all need to be monitored closely, since the licensing agencies will monitor them closely, too.

SETTING UP YOUR OFFICE

The first order of business is to make a space for your office. In a large center, this is much easier to do, since you can design an office space in the floor plans. With a home setting, it may prove quite challenging. You may need to be creative; your office may need to start out as a box, where all of the business papers, receipts, and forms are kept. If you do have a little more space, a file cabinet can house all the needed information for licensing purposes.

Office Necessities

A computer can make your business flow much smoother. The computer can store all the files used to print forms and correspondence and keep financial and payroll data.

A computer can be expensive if you are opening an in home center and do not already have one. The good news is that a portion of it can be written off at year's end as a business expense. The computer will also save you time. By setting up and using an accounting software program, your finances will always be in order. Using the software will not always guarantee the accounts are balanced, but it will show you where the money is coming in and where it is going.

Since the computer will be a time saver when figuring out taxes, receipts for your families, and so on, it will also save you money.

A receipt book is also necessary. When a family gives you their payment, whether it be weekly, bi-weekly, or monthly, they will need a receipt acknowledging how much they paid you for their tax purposes.

The usual supplies needed to run any business, such as paper, pens, paper clips, rubber bands, should be in your office. The larger your daycare operation is the more supplies you will need to keep on hand.

File folders or boxes are needed to store your receipts, health forms for the children, employee records, etc.

If you are a large center, you may consider having a fax machine, copy machine, or other such tools to save you from running to the office supply store to make copies or faxes.

MANAGING YOUR FINANCES

Your office could be filled with state of the art equipment and look immaculate.

Every supply is stocked, and you have pens and pencils to spare. But if you keep sloppy financial records, everything else is for naught. You need to be as meticulous in your budgeting, spending, and financial planning as you are in your business appearance.

Financial Planning

Once the basics are taken care of, you need to turn your attention to financial matters. The finances are literally what keep your operation afloat. When there is no money coming in, you get no money. Or worse there is money coming in, but with mismanagement and poor accounting, you do not know where it has gone. Keeping up to date records of all your numbers will benefit you greatly. Do not put off record keeping.

A ledger book will work for your accounting needs if you are a small center or an in home child care center. It is not recommended for larger centers for several reasons. One, it leaves open the opportunity for human calculation errors. Two, it takes much longer to figure out at the end of the year for tax reporting. Three, it is just not practical.

When you do have a small center, the ledger book will work if you are diligent. Enter all expenses, payments, and reimbursements as soon as they are received. Make copies of the receipts to keep them separated by month for easy access. If you are ever audited, the receipts marked by month will be much easier to find than digging through a stack of papers three feet high.

Make sure you know the balance of your books at any given moment. Do not let a pile of receipts or payments sit around. They could become lost or misplaced, throwing your whole balance off.

For any center, an accounting software program will keep track of your financial records. They can track profit and loss statements, they can keep track of budgets in several departments, and they can print receipts and invoices. They can also show you the balance in your accounts at all times. However, the software can only work when you enter the information accurately and promptly. Accounting software is no better than a ledger book if the receipts and invoices sit on the table collecting dust.

Budgeting

There are different types of budgeting that need to be done in different stages of your business. If you are in the building phase or planning process, you will need to create a startup budget. This budget is full of one-time purchases and estimates of what it will take to get your business up and fully functioning. These will include all major purchases of equipment such as tables, chairs, cribs, toys, outdoor toys, playpens, and office equipment. It can also include the first stocking of all your food, art, craft, educational program supplies, and toys.

A startup budget for a large center may be a huge expense. The U.S. General Accounting Office reports that the average startup costs for a child care center range from $8,000 to $90,000. If you have specialized equipment needs, such as for handicapped children, your expenses may be well over that number. And those figures do not take in to account the payroll or monthly expenses incurred with opening. This is what you need before you can even open your door.

If you do not have that kind of money, you can use an investor; they may handle some or all of the payments upfront. They may also be able to defer payments with creditors if they are an established investor or business. With having deferred payments, you can get some capital from opening and not rely on credit cards to finance your operations.

Once your child care business has opened, it will enter an operational budget phase. These are the costs of daily, weekly, and monthly operations. In order for your financial health to remain sound, you should have a budget for each area of your operation (and stick to it).

To make sure your financials are not in the red more than they are in the black, set up and follow a budget for each area of your child care center operations. This may be a little easier to do in a home, since there are fewer variables to plan. You know exactly how many kids are in your house for what meal and what supplies are on hand for projects. At large centers, the supplies will need to be well-stocked everyday to manage the volume of children you serve. The larger the volume, the larger the budget and the harder it is to plan.

Large centers may also require a board or corporate approval before any money can be spent. If the budget is not approved, you may have to rework your numbers until it is approved. A franchise will need to take each center's budget and make sure it fits within their own operating expenses before they can approve it.

Things You Need to Budget For

Food

A center that provides food will need to stay on top of the pantry supplies at all times. Ordering for a week or two ahead of time is advised, since shipment delays are always possible. You do not want to be without enough food to serve everyone.

The time of the year might also determine how much you spend. Fresh fruits and vegetables are much cheaper in season and will cost less. Even when they are off-season, if you belong to the food program, you need to keep providing these fruits and vegetables. Frozen and canned will work to some extent, but not for every occasion.

Monitor the food budget weekly. It could get out of control fast, toppling your whole expense report quickly. If one week goes over, see where you can cut the budget in a few places for the following week. If your budget is consistently blown in the food department, you may need to readjust. Your budget was not realistic, you did not estimate how much each child would eat correctly, or your food prices did not match compared to the suppliers. Whatever the reason, you need to adjust for the differences.

Insurance

This will also be a large chunk of your overall budget. As a business, you will be required to carry policies including fire protection and theft. An insurance agent who specializes in dealing with businesses can give you the best quote for one or all of the policies. The size and value of your center are taken in to account when figuring out the premium cost monthly.

Your center will be required to carry liability insurance. If you operate a home child care center, you may not be required to have liability insurance, but it is a good idea. That way, if something were to happen with your pet, on your property, or between children, you and your assets are protected. The amount of coverage you want will determine the price of your monthly premium.

Program Supplies

A child care center will need some type of supplies, even if you are not running a specific education program. The children will need something to do. There could be copying expenses for color pages or worksheets, art supplies, books, science project materials, etc. Allot a specific amount of money each week for supplies, and if you do not use it, let it carry over to the next week or fall into the general pot.

Educational Supplies

Depending on what type of program you do follow, you could incur some large expenses. Montessori pre-school and kindergarten programs are largely hands on, so they do not have expenses in copies and papers. However, they will need a lot of specialized materials. These materials will not be used up, but used over and over throughout the years. So much of it may be a one-time cost, or maintenance and updating fees over time.

Other programs require supplies such as books, art supplies, worksheets, and teacher materials. More and more pre-schools run some sort of academic program, and the children begin working with letters and numbers in depth. This requires workbooks or copying to be done by the teacher. Finding good workbooks and copying the pages for several years may be much more cost efficient for a small or home center.

Educational supply companies also offer discounts for teachers or centers who buy a large volume of products. In their catalogs, they offer tables, chairs, tools, books, workbooks, and everything needed for math, science, and social studies lessons for any age group. The only thing that will limit your program is your budget.

Training Costs

You will need to set up a monthly or annual budget for training purposes. The size of your staff will also determine the size and scope of this budget. Every state has different requirements on how many educational credits need to be earned every year. And every organization that offers approved classes will have a different fee. Over pad this budget a little, as the money left unused can always overflow in to the next year's education budget. One year you may have more new employees who need certification renewal or basic classes, costing a lot more money even though you have the same amount of staff.

Center Expenses

Just like a household, a business will need certain things to function. Those items are things such as a telephone, electricity, natural gas, water, sewer, garbage collection, and even Internet expenses. These payments could fluctuate slightly every month, depending on the climate, but they should be consistent from year to year. The center may be leased or rented and have a monthly rent payment. If it is a center that your or an investor built, there may be a mortgage payment each month.

Staffing

You need to budget your expected payroll expenses. There may be times when you are spending more on payroll, like when there is an employee turnover or you run a summer program and need additional staff. Always make sure that the profit outweighs the staffing expense in the bottom line. You need to at least meet the state requirements for student to staff ratios, but you do not need to go overboard.

Human Resources Benefits

If you are a large center, you may have to budget for more income than just payroll. Social security will require payments for every person you employ, including yourself. Large franchises offer full-time employees benefits, such as health care, vision, dental, and 401(k) plans. If you have enough profit margin, you can also budget those expenses in to your daily operations. By offering benefits, you will attract a higher quality of personnel and may not have to deal with the normally high turnover rate for childcare centers.

Marketing and Advertising

If your center is running at full capacity, you may not need to invest much in advertising. However, it is best to set aside some money in case you expand and do want a little publicity for your center. Costs for marketing vary for what medium you choose. Newspaper ads can run anywhere from $24 to $200 for one day. Color spots and feature placements in specialized circulars may cost several hundred dollars for one time ads. Other options for advertising include school newspapers, mailers, church newsletters, post cards, and a spot in a parade. Some of these routes may be free and others could cost thousands of dollars. Plan wisely before you agree to any advertising campaign. See Chapter 7 for more information on advertising your services.

Miscellaneous Expenses

Not every expense will be planned for ahead of time. There will be emergencies, special needs, and things that were overlooked. Some of these items include repairs and maintenance on your building. They may be costly if you are using an older building for your center. If it is your house, a portion of the repair cost may be written off at the end of the year.

Petty Cash

There is always an instance where you or someone in your employ will need a supply. When you have petty cash available, you can easily give the person cash up front and have them bring back a receipt. This is good for last minute purchases or items that were forgotten for a project, lunch, etc. Most petty cash systems work so that you can make purchases under $25. When it is over $25 (at a large center, anyway) your employee will need to purchase it and wait to be reimbursed or fill out a purchase agreement and wait for a check to be cut. When you opt for petty cash, if you have a receipt you can still track expenses. Replenish the petty cash so that when another need arises, you are not running to the bank first. Think of petty cash as an emergency fund.

Cost Control

Even with the best-laid budget in place, it can be spent and overspent quickly. If you have staff members with spending power, make sure they know the limits. Set up a program in your accounting software that tracks expenses for each type of budget. You can have an alert set up so you know when you are a certain amount away from reaching that goal. For instance, you can have a reminder sent when you are $500 away from the end of your food goal or you only have $25 left in the account for art supplies for the month. When you know you are close to the limit, you can take steps to ensure you do not go over your limit.

Keeping Supplies

With children in your regular care, you will need to anticipate their needs. Items to keep on hand will be diapers, wipes, cleaning products, food, formula, snacks, and program supplies. The higher the number of children you serve daily will require more supplies. How would your center run with a diaper shortage? Or how about a delay in milk? You need to be on top of your inventory and always be prepared for the worst-case scenarios.

Preparing for the worst-case scenario may sound pessimistic, but it could save you in the long run. Is your town isolated or far from another major town? Do winter driving conditions stop your deliveries from being on time? Is your region prone to natural disasters? If any of the above or other conditions could hamper supplies coming in to you, you need to make sure you always have several days' worth on hand.

Keep adequate food to feed everyone for two or three days during your good seasons. During the winter or harsh weather months, you may want to have at least a week's worth in the closet to anticipate delays. The food supplies needed include milk, formula, or baby food for every aged person attending your center.

Programs

When you have teachers for specific age groups, try and have them plan out the supplies they will need at least one week in advance. That way, they have the materials before they need them, and you can include them in your budgeting. If they are doing a science project and need four jars of baking soda, but your kitchen does not keep them in stock, you will need either to make a quick trip to the store or do without the activity. And what child likes to skip their fun activities?

Supplies to always keep on hand for the children includes scissors, colored paper, glue, play dough, foam shapes, pipe cleaners, and other decorative "items." Teachers and providers can be pretty creative if need be when concocting a project with few resources. It brings out your creativity, too.

Auditing

The word auditing elicits a severe reaction from most people. But if you keep good records, you have nothing to fear from the IRS. However, the state childcare licensing agency may have a say about it. Auditing is done on childcare centers not only for financial needs, but also to see if the center is maintaining the proper standards of care for the children.

An auditor will review your center's expenses and financial records. If you are an in home center, you probably will not have to do this. Hiring an auditor each year to look through your expenses and financial statements is an expense that you do not need when you are a small business.

If you are a large center or need to have your records audited, there are ways to make the process flow smoothly. Make sure all receipts are dated. If it is not clear what the item purchased was, write it at the top of the receipt. Keep track of who made what purchase. If you have multiple teachers in your employment, write what teacher it belongs to and if they were reimbursed. Store all invoices in one folder and place them in order of when they are due. Once they are paid, file them in a folder labeled the month they were paid. Keep a ledger or data file of all payments received from families, a running tab of their year to date payments and when they pay, and a monthly budget of what was spent and where.

Bookkeeping

Bookkeeping is not only needed for your finances, it is needed for your staff and children. Even though bookkeeping is an antiquated term, it pertains to records that can be kept on the computer. Bookkeeping is another way to help keep your business running smoothly since it will handle employee schedules, children's attendance records, staff attendance, injury reports, etc.

Attendance

Attendance should be taken daily and kept in a record on file if there are disputes later in the year. Human memory can be fallible at times, but if you have a record book or even an electronic sign in method, there will be little left to dispute.

Injury Reports

Injury reports are necessary for several reasons. They report what happened to the parents, they are kept on file in case an insurance agent ever needs to look at them, and you can see if a pattern of injuries develops. A pattern may mean several children getting a splinter from the wooden swing set week after week, signaling it needs to be replaced. Injury reports are also necessary to have as protection for your staff and your center in case a family tries to sue you for damages. The incidence report will clearly state what happened, who was involved, how it was resolved, and when.

An incident or injury report should be a triplicate form: one goes to the parent, one stays in the center, and another can be placed in the child's file. If you do not have triplicate forms, a report sheet can be copied after it has been filled out.

Staff

The child care business is open and running. You or your staff is providing the best care possible to one or many children. The staffing is going well, but you need to plan ahead and create back up plans for staffing. Home child care providers rely only on themselves for the day to day operations. However, they should have staffing back up plans, just as a large center would. What happens if you get sick? What happens if your child gets sick? What if there is a family emergency? A home child care provider especially needs to have an assistant or a back up person who is licensed to care for the children in the home when the normal provider cannot do so.

A home child care provider should have at least one back up person to call in case of an emergency. This person or these persons should have all the necessary requirements, such as CPR certification, first aid training, and the medical testing needed to be legal and licensed to run a child care operation.

Ratios

The employees of a medium to large sized center will be diverse. They will not always be easy to schedule and manage either. You will need to consider the size of your center before you can determine the size of your staff.

For each age group of children, there is a state mandated ratio of adults to children. Most states break down the age groups the following way:

Infant: 0 to 9 months

Toddler: 9 to 18 months

Older Toddler: 18 to 24 months

Preschool: 24 months to 48 months

School aged: 48 months and older

The majority of states require one adult for every three infants with normal needs. When a child with special needs is present in your center, you may need a lower ratio. The special needs child may also need one on one staffing.

Toddlers are a little bit older and a little bit more dependent. The ratio for this age group is usually three to four toddlers per adult caregiver.

Older toddlers can have between four or five children per every adult caregiver.

Preschoolers have even higher ratios, and are allowed between four and six children for every adult in the room.

School aged children have the highest ratios since they are the most independent, and can have anywhere from six to ten children for every adult present.

Scheduling

In the day to day operations, children will be sick, go on vacation, or stay with another family member. Even though an age group or your home limits may not be met, you need to have enough staff scheduled every day in case there is. Say, for example, you have a surprise visit from an inspector. You knew there might be a few kids on vacation since it was near the Fourth of July holiday, and a staff person wanted the day off, too. You anticipated there would be enough children to excuse this staff member without replacing him or her, but guess what? The children all showed up and the staff member was gone. While you are scrambling to cover the spot, the inspector walks in and finds one of your rooms way understaffed. You would be written up and the violation placed in your records.

On the other hand, the staff member could have requested the day off. You were not sure how many children would be in that room for the day, so you scheduled a substitute in their place. Thank goodness you did, because all of the children showed up. If this were the scenario, the inspector would see your staffing is adequate and be on their way.

Scheduling will also become a toss up against your profit statement. Is it financially wise to hire fewer employees and give them more hours or hire multiple people at part-time status? If you do not offer benefits to full-time employees, it may then only be a preference in dealing with people over the cost.

The Pros of Hiring Full-Time and Offering Benefits to Employees:

- Employee satisfaction
- Lower turnover rate
- Higher quality of applicants for the jobs
- Higher quality of care for the children
- Less staff to train, manage, and schedule
- Less people for the families to ask questions of
- More one on one care for children

The Cons of Hiring Full-Time and Offering Benefits to Employees:

- Benefits are expensive
- Benefits are not a guarantee to higher quality applicants
- Full-time employees require more vacation/time off

The Pros of Offering Part-Time Employment

- Many more people to work with in scheduling
- More flexibility to have substitutes and cover for illnesses

The Cons of Offering Part-Time Employment

- Less applicants to choose from since many people need full-time work
- Lower quality of applicants

- Higher turnover rate as part-time employees find full-time work and benefits
- More people to train, manage, and schedule
- More people for the children to listen to, becoming confusing

As a larger child care center, you can mix it up with full-time and part-time positions. The full-time positions are ideal for people, usually women, who want to work outside of the home. The part-time positions are ideal for students who are attending school for teaching or childcare careers. Scheduling can turn sour when students continually ask for time off to study or for exams, mid-term breaks, or even absenteeism. And if the student is attending school while living away from home, they may not be able to work year round.

The problem of absenteeism is not one only for students. Adults of any age may have a problem with absenteeism. They will need to have substitutes in place to maintain the ratio of the class.

FORMS FOR REPORTING AND RECORDING

Every agency that monitors businesses will require a paper trail. With a child care center, the paper work required to open and stay open is extensive. Not only do you need paperwork on yourself and your business, but you will need it for all of the children and any staff members in your presence. If the correct papers are not filled out or up to date, your license could be in jeopardy.

Standard Health Form

Every child in attendance will need a medical sheet filled out by a doctor. This health form basically lists any allergies, special needs, or difficulties the child may have. If there are special needs or health concerns, the health form will also describe what special care will be required to handle that child.

Immunization Records

Immunizations are very important amongst young children to keep sicknesses and diseases to a minimum. In large centers, an immunization record filled out by the doctor will need to be kept on file. This file will also need to be updated yearly as the child grows or moves in to other rooms. An in home center can monitor the immunizations easily since the caregiver will likely know what day the child is leaving to get the shots. The immunization record can be given so it is updated that same day.

Employee Information

Employees will require a sheet with all their information such as job history, medical conditions, limitations, emergency contact info, etc.

Employee Health Form

Employees will also need to have a physical by a doctor and get a clean bill of health before working. This health sheet will list any physical limitations and special equipment needed for the person to complete their job satisfactorily.

Emergency Contact Information

Emergency contact sheets will need to be kept on all staff members and children within your center. Several phone numbers, cell phone numbers, and addresses of people should be kept on hand in case of a health, weather, or security issue.

See the resource section for sample forms that are ready for use.

"There are no seven wonders of the world in the eyes of a child. There are seven million."

~ Walt Streightiff

11
ACCREDITATION & EDUCATION

If you want to enlist an educational program within your child care center, you can investigate accreditation policies. Accreditation is a national set of guidelines, which are voluntary for anyone caring for young children, that dictate what and how to teach young children. If you implement all their policies and plans, you must go through an application process to accredit your center.

The National Association for the Education of Young Children (NAEYC) is the national governing body for accreditation. They provide education and support for those centers that are accredited and educate others on the importance of getting accredited. The NAEYC has created a system for applying and getting accredited. They have also set forth a fee structure for the accreditation process, which is four steps. The cost of each step is determined by the size of the center you are trying to have accredited. The NAEYC categorizes centers by size from 10 to 60 children, 61 to 120, 121 to 240, 241 to 360, and in increments of 120.

ACCREDITATION PROCESS

Enrollment

The first step in accreditation is enrollment. Enrollment fees begin at $425 and go up to $775 or higher if you have over 360 children in your child care center or school. Enrollment is the process of filling out an enrollment form and beginning a self study of your center. During the self study, you learn about the eligibility requirements, identify your strengths and weaknesses, and improve your center so it meets the requirements.

Application

The application process begins when the enrollment self study is completed. The fees range from $200 to $425. During the application step, the person involved in the self study signs off that they believe the applying center meets the eligibility requirements set forth by the NAEYC. The application will also need to have a date chosen for which all materials will be turned in. After you have been approved as an applicant, you will be given a formal self study to look for specific items within your curriculum.

The NAEYC gives you a self assessment workbook in which you go step by step through your processes, document them, and make copies to turn in with your materials. The application process takes several months.

Candidacy

Once all the materials are sent to the NAEYC, the center becomes a candidate for accreditation. This step is billed in conjunction with the on site visit, and the fees range from $650 to $1,175.

During the candidacy stage, your center is preparing for the onsite visit. Self analysis and performance improvement is key during this time to make sure you do meet all the eligibility requirements for accreditation.

On Site Visit

The on site visit usually occurs within six months of the initial enrollment. A representative from NAEYC will come to your site and see if you meet the requirements necessary to attain accreditation. To do so, you will need to pass on at least 80 percent of the core areas set forth by the requirement materials. After the visit, the representative will either grant or deny your status as accredited. If you are accredited, the licensure will last five years. After that time, you will need to reapply. If you are not granted accreditation, you can reapply after a certain time.

Annual Report

The annual report is sent out by the NAEYC and lists centers that are accredited. It also discusses any changes made during the year or any policies that will be implemented. This phase ranges in cost from $300 to $450.

The Pros of Accreditation

- The practice of getting accredited means you are entitled to state and federal monies to help run your program. Every little bit of money you can receive for equipment and supplies will help your bottom line. Grant and project money can keep you from having to take out another loan, seek more private financing, or even go without the supplies until you can get the money.

- Parents will also know that you follow a set curriculum plan for proper education and development. The label of accreditation on your center, no matter how large or small it is, tells people you know what to teach and how to teach young children effectively.

- Accreditation can earn you business. Many in home and smaller centers do not bother with getting accreditation since there is paperwork to be filed and yearly updates to learn. When you advertise, you can declare you are state accredited and that will earn you business on that fact alone.

- If you hire a staff member who does not have a formal teaching degree, the state will have guidelines for them to follow. The state may also supply resources such as worksheets, pamphlets, and activities for children to do.

- Being an accredited school will get you listed on the national accreditation site. When families are searching for a care giver, they may run across your accredited center and call. This is free publicity.

The Cons of Accreditation

- The cost of becoming accredited can be very expensive, especially if you are a small center.

- The steps required to become accredited can be lengthy and time consuming, sometimes taking over a year to complete.

- Different types of programs may also require different types of accreditation. For instance, preschool programs do not require as much programming as a kindergarten or Montessori program will. Montessori is a separate program that uses educational practices set forth by Maria Montessori, and is very popular. You will need to attend a special training school to be able to call yourself a Montessori school and earn Montessori accreditation.

- Becoming accredited may help your business. You will need to weigh the pros and cons and see if it makes sense for you. An in home person with only six children is not able to apply for accreditation.

Other Accreditation

Since preschool education is becoming increasingly popular, the National Association for Family Child Care (NAFCC) has created its own set of accreditation guidelines. They are the only agency that allows for a family child care provider to be accredited. This accreditation focuses on families and relationships within the home child care system.

The accreditation is voluntary, but proves to parents that the caregiver is committed to providing a secure, nurturing, and safe environment for their child to grow in.

The process of being accredited with NAFCC is much easier and affordable for in home caregivers. To begin with, there is a list of eligibility requirements, which include:

1 – You must be in home and spend 80 percent of your day time hours caring for children.

2 – You need to be at least 21 years old.

3 – You need to have graduated from high school or have a GED.

4 – You must care for children in your home for a minimum of 15 hours.

5 – You must complete a background screening.

6 – You need at least three children enrolled in your care, with at least one of them having an address other than your home. They must also be present for an observation.

7 – You must have 18 months minimum of experience running your child care center.

If you meet all the criteria, you can fill out an application and begin the process. When you mail in your application, you also mail in the fee. If you are a member of NAFCC, the fee is $495. Nonmembers can still apply, and the fee is $695. Once your paperwork is processed, you will be sent a self study to examine your program. The self study will direct you on what to do and how to implement the program in to your daily care. A member will perform an observation of your center and make any recommendations to you. The entire process takes several months to a year or more to complete.

Child Development Associate (CDA)

If you do not necessarily want to pursue accreditation for your center, you can pursue it for yourself. The Council for Professional Recognition was created in 1985 to improve and recognize employees in the early childhood education industry. They administer what is called the Child Development Associate (CDA) credentialing program.

It is very important for child care providers to be educated on all things relating to children in health, development, and well being. Classes were designed to improve education, and then given a point value by the system. For example, one day long class teaching behavior strategies is worth two Continuing Education Units (CEUs), which go toward your CDA. In certain states, you are required to have so many CEUs every year to keep your license current. Failure to attend training and classes to earn CDA credit can harm the status of your license.

The rules regarding CDA requirements for in home and large centers are different. Some states require everyone who works at the large center to have a minimum of three CEUs per year to remain employed. However, an in home provider may need to have at least six every year to keep their license. There is not a national standard for training levels, but in future years, there may be as the council is working towards standardizing the requirements.

Further education can come in the form of an associate's or bachelor's degree. Community colleges, online training schools, and vocational schools all offer programs in child care training. The type of school you choose to attend will determine how long your training program is. A community college offering an associate's degree in child care will probably take two years to complete. A college or university that offers a bachelor's degree in child development will probably take at least four years to earn. A vocational or trade school might offer a training program where you get a certificate of completion or CEU credits.

"Remember that children, marriages, and flower gardens reflect the kind of care they get."

~ H. Jackson Brown, Jr.

12
CHILDREN'S POLICIES

The heart of your child care business is the children. You will need activities for each age group to keep them occupied and to cover a multitude of developmental milestones. Not only do the children need playtime, they need structure and routine to help them develop into well adjusted adolescents.

SAMPLE SCHEDULE

A preschool aged child does not need a rigid schedule, but a loose one will help them through the progression of the day and aid them with transitions. A home child care center or a young preschool class can benefit by creating a simple schedule and loosely following it. Every day will have its challenges and the schedule will need to be adapted for those days, but on average, you should stick to it as close as possible.

7 to 8:30	Children arrive
8:30 to 9:15	Play time
9:15 to 9:30	Clean up, bathroom break (diaper change)
9:30 to 9:45	Circle time

9:45 to 10:30	Centers
10:30 to 11:15	Outdoor play or indoor free play
11:15 to 11:30	Read books
11:30 to 11:45	Bathroom, wash hands, lunch prep
11:45 to 12:30	Lunch
12:30 to 1:00	Clean up, books, bathroom
1:00 to 2:45	Nap
2:45 to pickup	Outdoor play, indoor play, free time, etc.

Circle Time

Circle time is good for children who have turned three-years-old. Traditionally, it is called "circle" time because the students sit in a circle on the floor around the teacher or caregiver. The circle time is spent in a mini lesson structured around a lesson plan, story, or other activity that falls within your educational program guidelines. Circle times include reading a book, learning a lesson, seeing a demonstration, or sharing with each other. Circle time is introduces young students to sitting and developing an attention span. Circle times should be small amounts of time for young children and gradually turn into longer periods determined by their age.

Centers

Centers are individualized tasks that can be related to the day's circle time or be independent, but related to learning. Several centers can be run at one time, allowing the children to participate in one, but switch to another, allowing them all a chance with each center. For example, each center may last 15 minutes approximately. One center is finger painting a picture, another center is practicing writing the letter "B," and the last center is drawing a picture about the story they read in circle time. The children are split up evenly and sent to a center; after fifteen minutes, they rotate to another one. Centers are usually only done in larger child care settings where there is enough staff to handle each center.

Show and Tell

Show and tell is a great opportunity for children to grow. Showing and telling is a way to get children used to speaking in front of their peers, sharing parts of their life, and taking turns. Not every young child will like to share a show and tell item, but give them the opportunity to do so. After several weeks of watching their friends, they may come around and decide to participate. Not all children have a problem with shyness, but for those that do, show and tell gives them a chance to develop speaking skills, as well as self-esteem and confidence.

Play Time

Play time is very important in the development of children. While they do need some structure and rules as far as behavior, they also need time to just be. Letting them have free time and playing with what they choose for a large portion of the day, everyday, is just as important to their development as trying to teach them all day long. Actually, free play would probably work better since keeping the attention of a three-year-old all day long on one topic would be tough if not impossible.

INDOOR PLAYTIME

While they have "free" playtime, you can have different activities out and ready for them. Or you can simply let the children wander about the room until they find something that interests them and they want to play. Indoor time should have limited TV viewing time. A movie can be put on to entertain the children while you are preparing lunch or changing the other children's diapers; this is completely acceptable. However, having the TV "baby-sit" the child all day long is not.

Gym and Gymnastics

If your center is large enough, set aside a large room and make it an activity room. Have a parachute to play with as a group. The children develop large and small motor skills when they work together to raise and lower the parachute. They can also work in teams. One team is shaking the parachute up and down trying to get foam balls off while the other team is trying to get all of the balls on the parachute.

A large room can also have mats in place on the floor and large foam cushions for rolling and gymnastic type activities. Rolling, tumbling, jumping, and skipping are great ways to develop large motor skills and have regular exercise. And when the children have exercise, they expend energy and might not get so restless or bored.

Crafts

Arts and crafts projects are always fun and can be tailored to each age group. Crafts are important in developing fine motor skills, such as cutting, grasping, pinching, and holding a crayon or marker. The basic supplies to keep on hand are glue, scissors, colored paper, crayons, markers, paint, and paintbrushes. Extra supplies to purchase when your budget allows would be glitter, googly eyes, feathers, foam pieces, jingle bells, and wood sticks.

Craft projects can be as simple as finger-painting a piece of paper or as elaborate as designing a 3-D project. The only limitation is your supplies or your budget to buy those supplies.

Finding project ideas is easy. When you have children who are already in school, you can imitate art projects they bring home. You can also stock up on art project idea books at the educational store. If you do not have a library of craft books, visit a public library to get ideas for projects. Online Web sites have a host of places to look for craft projects, too. You can search by material, age, holiday, or complexity. See the resource section for a list of Web sites with great project ideas.

Art projects can be done once a day or once a week. If you run an in home center and have only infants or toddlers, art may be extra hard to accomplish on a daily basis. Scheduling art is important as it also gets them used to different textures and sensations. They learn to get messy, how to get clean, what paint feels like, what glue feels like, and what it feels like to be clean again.

Puzzles

Puzzles are another great developmental tool for children. Puzzles can come in large pieces and be made to put together on the floor. As the children grow and develop more critical thinking skills, they can handle smaller puzzle pieces and puzzles with a larger number of pieces. These puzzles may be the kind to put together within a frame or they may be without a set frame. There is virtually no limit to the type and style of puzzles you can buy.

Play Dough

Even though some activities made for the indoors can get messy, they are important. Play dough is one such tool. Being able to manipulate the play dough into forms helps hand eye coordination, as well as fine motor skills. The working of the play dough also increases hand strength and gets the child used to different sensory feelings.

Many different tools and accessories are available to go along with play dough. You can cut it into pieces, roll it flat like a pancake, or make it into smaller pieces. Cookie cutters are great to use for making shapes and characters in play dough.

To keep the play dough mess to a minimum, use it on a table over a hard wood or linoleum floor. This way, any pieces that drop to the floor can be easily picked up and reused. If you only have carpeting in your room or center, try placing a plastic mat under the table for protection. If no plastic mat is available, you have a couple of options. Pick up as much of the play dough as possible and reuse if it is not filled with dirt or hair. Whatever remains in the carpet can be picked up with a knife later on when it is dry and can be scraped. A vacuum will also work over the dried play dough.

Games

Kids love to play any type of game you can make up. Whether it is Duck Duck Goose or Red Rover they like the structured activity. Games can come in the form of large group, physical activities. These include Duck Duck Goose, Ring around the Rosie, Farmer in the Dell, Tag, Sharks and Fish, and so on. They can be done outdoors or inside in a large room.

Other games can be large group, non-physical in nature. This could be I Spy, Hot Potato, Musical Chairs, etc. Large group games can be done in a circle type setting or during the winter or bad weather when outdoor play is not an option.

Small groups can include props. You can play hide the thimble with a small group.

Music

Music is another great activity for children. No matter how old they are, they can listen to music. The older they are, the better they will participate. They can sing along, play musical instruments, or even a musical game. The library or the Internet will also have lists of games you can play.

OUTDOOR PLAYTIME

Field Trips

If you will be opening a larger center, field trips are a great way to explore your surrounding area. Even if you do not have transportation capabilities, parents can be responsible for getting the child to and from the destination. Field trips can be anywhere: an apple farm, a zoo, a wildlife preserve, a museum, a park, a factory, or anywhere you think the children would enjoy. See the policy section in this chapter on handling fieldtrips.

If you will have a summer program for school aged children, a movie may be a fun place to visit once a week. Any type of event where they can participate, like bowling, swimming, climbing, or gymnastics is also fun and low cost. When you have field trips, charge a small fee that will cover each child and any transportation costs. Field trips with smaller fees are much more popular than those that carry high price tags.

Parties

Any place that has children will need parties. You can offer celebrations for Halloween, Thanksgiving, Christmas, Easter, and Valentine's Day. You could always observe Hanukkah and Kwanzaa. If you are open year round, there is Memorial Day, Labor Day, and the Fourth of July.

If you cannot observe any of the Christian or religious holidays, have a fall, winter, spring, and summer festival. Each one can have special foods, crafts, and songs to celebrate the passing of the new season. The children do not care what it is; they just like parties.

Birthdays can also be observed with a party. With a small or home center, you can make a cake for the child. You could also play some games and let them choose what they want to do on their "special" day. Some parents will provide a cake or all of the treats – you just need to check in with them ahead of time.

CHILDREN'S ISSUES

Besides the fun and games with children, you will be faced with serious problems, too. To handle these situations promptly, you need to be adequately prepared and make sure your staff is trained to handle any of the following problems if and when they arise.

Sick Policy

Children are not known as being germ mongers for nothing. To prevent constant sickness from invading your home, you will need to have and enforce a rigid sickness policy. If you are a large center, providing sick rooms may even be an extra service that you offer. However, unless you can afford a sick room, you will need to ban students who are not having normal, child health issues.

A typical sick policy will read like this:

Children may not enter the center if they have shown any signs of the following during the preceding 24-hour period:

- Fever of 100 degrees or higher
- Vomiting
- Green, runny nose
- Rashes or unidentified sores
- Diarrhea
- Hives or allergic reactions
- Sore throat
- Fainting or dizzy spells
- No appetite
- Convulsions
- Extreme lethargy

These may sound obvious, but you might be surprised by what a parent may try to cover up. A child care provider in Michigan had a three-year-old in her care who only attended part time. Even though he was part time, the days his mother worked were not flexible and she could not take any time off. One day, she came in carrying him, and he immediately said he was sick. The mother corrected him and said, "You were in the night, but you are better now." The provider questioned what happened, just to be on the safe side. The mother said the child simply ate too much apple for his evening snack and had thrown up during the night. The provider was nice and offered her the benefit of the doubt and let him stay. But he continued to vomit all morning and exposed the other children. When the grandmother picked him up, she explained further that he had thrown up all night and not just once. However, the mother failed to provide this information.

When the symptoms are diagnosed by a doctor and medicine is prescribed, you will still need to limit the child's attendance. Standard policies allow a child back into your care after they have been on antibiotics for 24 to 48 hours. You will need to use your discretion if it is something like an ear infection that is not contagious to the other children.

Medicine Dispensing Policy

Any time a child has a prescription medicine, a permission slip will be required from the parent for you to dispense it to the child. A permission slip should include the name of the medicine, what it is for, when it is to be given, and the dosage amount. The slip should include when the medicine should begin and when the medicine should end for each child. A parent signature is required. On the back of the slip is a checklist to write the date and time of each dose given. See the resource section for an example of a medicine permission slip.

Special Medical Conditions

Many childhood illnesses and diseases may need you to create a special policy. For instance, many children suffer from PKU, which prevents them from having any form of food with phenylalanine in it. They require a specialized diet. Other children have severe asthma and require breathing treatments during the day. Children may have diabetes, cystic fibrosis, gluten intolerance, and ADD. Every condition has special needs, but you can create a policy to ensure your safety and theirs before you agree to any type of care. These instances are rare, but can happen.

Head Lice

A head lice infestation will make everyone scratch. Head lice are a very common childhood ailment and one that is very contagious. To keep head lice out of your center or from spreading, you need a rigid policy.

If it is discovered a child has head lice or head lice nits in their hair while at the center, they will need to immediately go home. You can instill a nit free policy that states they are not allowed to return until their head is nit free. Perform the check yourself to be absolutely sure there are no nits. You can also set a minimum number of days before they are allowed to return, such as two, three, or even five days. Still perform a check, even if it has been the allotted number of days, and declare them nit free before returning them to their class.

When nits are found on a student's head, whether in your center or at home, you should check your whole operation. Chances are they might already be in several other children's hair. Line the children up and check each head separately with a toothpick or fine comb to look for nits or adult head lice. Follow the same procedure for each child that is found to have any in their hair. Call their parents, send them home with instructions on getting rid of the lice, and then permit them to return when they are nit free.

Having head lice and head lice infestations may make you feel dirty. However, it is important to remember several things about head lice. They prefer clean environments. They love clean and shiny hair, and they can affect anybody. Children who get head lice may feel bad and get picked on by the other children. Keep their feelings in mind when discussing any issues of head lice in your center or home. If possible, keep it confidential about who has it and who was sent home. A stigma attached to a child can stick for a long time and hurt their esteem.

Preventing head lice in your center is almost impossible. You can take steps so that children do not share headwear, nap items, or clothing, but they are in close quarters all day. An infestation can happen and spread with even the best of care.

Cleaning up after a head lice or nit infestation will take some time. The following should be done to sanitize all areas in your care:

- Wash all bedding in hot water.

- Place all stuffed animals in trash bags and place in the freezer or outdoors in freezing weather for at least 24 hours.

- Wash or freeze all toys and dress up clothing such as hats, scarves, glasses, and helmets that come in contact with a child's head.

- Wash or vacuum all sleeping surfaces such as beds, mattresses, cots, and pillows.

- If pillows cannot be washed, place them in trash bags in the freezer or place outdoors for 24 hours.

When an outbreak occurs, you will need to inform every family in your care about their exposure to head lice. Make the note short but informative.

FAMILY INFORM NOTE

Dear Parent,

Head lice have been found in our center (or my home). I have checked your child for head lice and nits and have not found anything. Please be aware of this and continue to check and keep your child nit free. If head lice are found in your child, they will need to be kept out of school until they are nit free. Please call me if you have any questions.

Sincerely,

Provider Name

Remember that head lice are not a disease, but a nuisance. It is only one of the few drawbacks of working with children. See the resource section in the back for links to head lice infestation "cures."

Allergies

Childhood allergies are becoming more and more prevalent today. Not only are kids allergic to things outdoors, but they are sensitive to certain foods. Certain foods even trigger allergic reactions that are harmful and fatal if not caught and treated immediately. When you have a child with allergies in your care, it should be noted on their medical information card. Any special treatments or medications and the dosage should be listed on the card. In the case of severe allergies, special considerations should take place.

Limited Outdoor Activities

A child may have such severe allergies that they are not allowed to go outside during peak allergen times. When ragweed breaks out in the fall or when mold counts are highest in the spring and on rainy days, a child may need to stay indoors. Provide other activities for them to do with another caregiver while their class goes outside. If you are in a home child care center, everyone will have to stay in since the children cannot be separated and away from the supervision of an adult.

Food Precautions

Peanuts cause some of the scariest and most dangerous reactions among children. Peanut allergies can cause breathing problems, vomiting, swelling, nausea, and anaphylaxis shock. When a child has an allergy that is that severe, they will need to have an EPI pen with them or on site at all times.

An EPI pen is an emergency medication inside of a needle. It is a shot with a medicine that immediately counterattacks the allergen. When anaphylaxis shock occurs, the EPI pen will need to be administered immediately, and the paramedics will need to be called. The parents' need to be called and alerted to the event and told that medical help is on the way. The child will probably need to go to the hospital and be given other medications to get their body back to normal.

Preventing Food Allergy Reactions

Special care will be needed for all food preparations in the presence of a food allergen. Some allergies are so sensitive that even if they breathe the scent of the food, they have a reaction. When that is the case, the food will need to be eliminated from the menu. A letter will need to be sent home to all the parents notifying them of the food banishment. Snacks and other food that contain the offending food cannot be shared as a treat or snack anytime, anywhere.

The down side to limiting food is just that, a limit. If the allergy is so bad that the air can trigger a reaction, you may need to consider your alternatives. Say the allergic reaction was just to the smell of peanuts. That would mean that no peanut butter or peanut products could enter your house or center, by any means. No staff members could have peanut butter in their lunches from home, no one in the center could have peanut butter sandwiches, peanut butter cookies, or peanut treats. Peanut butter is a staple in some people's diets. How can you expect the whole center to comply with the demands of one person? You may find other families are not happy about the policy if you enforce it and keep the child in your care.

If the allergen entered the home or center care by accident, you may have a liability issue on your hands if the child has a severe or anaphylaxis reaction. It may be a situation where it is best to let them go or have them find another means of care rather than disrupt your whole household or center.

Other Allergy Causes

Peanuts are not the only food allergy to remember while you are cooking. There are children who are allergic to eggs, milk, dairy products, any kind of nut, strawberries, red dye, citrus products, aspartame, and glutens. When all these children require special diets, you may think you are going nuts. In order to be efficient as a provider and not spend your day making specialty dishes, the parents may need to bring in foods that agree with their dietary restrictions.

Child Abuse or Neglect

Sometimes children live in households where their best interests are not observed. As a child care provider, you are required to report any activity you suspect to be illegal to the proper authorities. Some of these actions may include physical, mental, or sexual abuse. The child may also speak of activity in the house that includes drugs, weapons, or sexual activity. You are legally bound to report any obvious signs of harm to the child.

If the signs are not obvious, you may need to investigate further. If the child has no bruises, but says they are hurting in a lot of places, time and again, keep a logbook for that child. Document what the child says, when it happened, and to whom they reported it to. Some children are too young to fully understand what is happening to them and will not be able to accurately tell what is going on. Other children are storytellers and like to fabricate tales. You will have to determine what the child's personality is and deem an appropriate response.

Child abuse and neglect may be very obvious. They may show up with bruises, say they are being left home alone, or say they have been inappropriately touched. When they do so, you are required to call social services immediately for the child to be investigated.

Abuse and neglect may also be very subtle. A child facing abuse may act out in ways that could be termed immature or just a phase, even though they have never acted that way before. Talking to a child and asking what is going on in their life may be the best way to find answers. And if you suspect something, you can always ask a parent. Bring it to their attention by saying, "Susie has been behaving strangely during the last few weeks. She is unusually aggressive and sad during the day. Is there something unusual going on at home?" This way, you are not accusing the parent of anything; you are simply raising a concern. There may not be abuse or neglect, but a simple developmental change going on within the child. Either way, the parent can discuss it with their child and then work to take the appropriate action. If no action is taken by the parent, and the situation becomes worse or more obvious, you can call in social services to investigate.

Potty Training

This time in a child's life both brings out the best and worst of an adult. You are thrilled they are growing older and in control of their bodies, but frustrated if the process does not run as smoothly as you think it should. Being a child care provider, you will need to work closely with the parents to determine when you think a child is ready for toilet training.

The luxury of decision making will not always include you. You may care for the child 50 plus hours every week, but one morning a parent may show up and announce they have begun the potty training process. They did not consider you, your daily schedule, or what your thoughts were on the child's willingness to learn, but you are forced to comply nonetheless. They are the parent and you must respect their wishes. You can state your disagreement or even agreement with the parent, and work through your policy.

In your toilet training policy, you may need to set limits not only for your time, but also hygiene and cost. A smaller, home child care center will offer more flexibility in toilet training, since fewer children need the bathroom, and there is one caregiver to provide consistent encouragement. However, accidents do happen. If accidents keep happening, you may need to discuss going back to diapers for a while until the child is ready. To keep any disputes to a minimum, use a number to set the expectations for everyone. For example, Susie is having four or more accidents every day. Not only is the child disappointed in what her parents perceive as "failure," there is the issue of soiled clothing to deal with. Who is doing all of the laundry? Is the family bringing adequate supplies of clean clothing? When there is soiled clothing, the chances for an accident to happen on the floor or furniture is great, too.

When a family insists on using pull-ups as a part of their training plan, have them provide the pull-ups. You may provide the diapers and get them at a discount, but pull-ups are much more expensive than diapers, especially if there are numerous accidents during the day. If they do not agree, simply state it is your policy, and they need to comply or do something else, such as bring underwear or revert to diapers, until the child appears more ready.

Nap Time

Nap time is every parent's and childcare provider's dream, for a few minutes anyway. You will need to set up a policy about nap time procedures, but allow for a little flexibility. A good policy for nap time would include the ages of the children who still get naps and the time during which they can nap.

Example: All children under three-years-old will be given nap time during 12:30 and 2:30.

Considerations in nap time flexibility will include the parent's wishes. They might not want their child to have a nap because then they stay up too late or then they do not get up on time. Make a special form on your caregiver contract stating you will not give that specific child naps unless the parents request it. The child can do other quiet activities during that time.

And remember that just because it is nap time, does not mean a child will sleep. At a large center, it is difficult for children to fall asleep, simply because of the number of bodies in one close area. And other children do go to bed early and not have to get up early, so they may not need naps. What you may do for these children is offer quiet activities while remaining in their designated sleeping area. Hand them several books to read to themselves while the other children sleep. Give them an easy puzzle or two to do while everyone else sleeps. As long as you offer resting time, the child should be quiet so that others can sleep even if they cannot.

Child Release Policies

With child abductions on the increase, you need to do everything in your power to prevent them. Enforcing certain safeguards will not only protect the children, but they will protect you in the long run. Create a strict policy on who is allowed to pick up a child. Enforce this policy. It only takes one mishap, and disasters can happen.

Every child should have an information sheet that lists who is authorized to pick them up. When someone comes to pick up the child and they are not on the sheet, the child will not go home with them.

Other actions to include on your child release policy:

- Require parents to inform you in writing if someone other than mom or dad will be picking up the child and when.
- The person who is picking up the child will need to present a valid picture ID.
- The person picking the child up must be included on your child release list.

If any of the above requirements are not met, the child does not leave. Place a phone call to mom or dad and let them know you did not release the child and why. Verbal permission over the phone will need to be used at your discretion if there was a mix up.

Child Safety

To go along with keeping kids safe and inside your center, you may want to have a special lock installed on your entrance doors. This special lock requires a code that must be used to get inside. This three or four digit code must be typed in to the doorknob or else entry will be denied. Using the coded doorknobs will keep unwanted solicitors away, as well as parents who do not have visiting or custodial rights with their child or just plain old criminals. The doorknob provides safety to everyone in the center, not just to the children. This may not be practical in home child care centers, but locking the door is just as effective. You will only need to unlock and open it each time a child's parent arrives to pick them up.

When the children play outside, have them play in a contained area. A large, fenced in yard is ideal, but not always practical. If you have a large yard, it may be too expensive to fence it all in. When it is too expensive, consider fencing in a portion that can be used as a play area.

Large fenced in areas will keep all the children inside, but they still need to be monitored closely. Know where the gates are and keep them locked. A one-way entry door can keep unwanted people out, as well as a key coded padlock. Keeping intruders and unwanted people out of the outside play areas is just as important as keeping them out of the inside play areas.

Dismissal Policy

Dismissing a child or a family from your care may be a difficult and emotional but necessary action. In order to remove someone from your care, you need to have adequate reason and documented paperwork to do so.

Some reasons for dismissal may include:

- **Failure to pay** — A family may have hit a financial hardship and has not paid for several weeks, but continues to bring their children to you. Offer written notice that they need to make arrangements to reconcile their account or future care will be terminated. Give them a deadline. If the deadline is not met, send a termination notice. Make the time frame reasonable, to accommodate working schedules, but not overly lenient. If you show leniency, they will continue to abuse the policy, and you will never get paid. Keep copies of your notices and warnings in case they try to sue you for wrongful termination.

- **Behavioral issues** — Citing behavioral problems for dismissal can be tricky. You need to prove that the behavior is exceptionally out of the norm and you and or your staff cannot handle it. Behavioral dismissal simply cannot be due to normal development stages and lack of maturity.

Issues that can fall under abnormal behavior:

- **Excessive biting** — All children have a phase in the toddler years when they are teething and bite. When the biting moves from objects to children, it becomes a problem. If the child remains young and does it occasionally, it is excusable. When the child reaches three, four, or older and continues to bite, dismissal may be appropriate. You will need to go through a warning system, which encourages the parents to work with you, to stop the behavior, or get to the reason why it is still occurring. Biting may be due to a child who does not know how to communicate and needs some direction in how to do so. Biting may stem from excessive teething pain. Biting may also come from frustration in a home environment. Either way, parents of the other child(ren) that keep getting bit will not be happy. You will need to assure them you are working to remedy the situation and that you care about the health of all children involved.

- **Caregiver conflicts** — If there is a conflict between a child and a person on your staff, you will need to do some investigatory work. Does a child have more problems that are usual with a particular staff member? Is the staff member antagonizing the child? Does the child not comply with group direction, following instruction, or listen when they need to? You may need to counsel both parties, as one incident may have sparked the problem. For example, the staff member may have been too friendly and lenient towards a child one day when the toys needed to be picked up; therefore, their authority is no longer respected by the child. Or a staff member may have disciplined the child too harshly and now the child is afraid of that person. Dismissing a child from caregiver conflicts is rare, but always a possibility.

In your home child care operation, you may have a child that is just out of sorts with your method. Do they not listen to you? Do they cause problems for the other children? Is there any underlying cause to their problem, such as an undiagnosed allergy, a disease that is untreated, or simply authority problems? You will need to investigate to make sure there is a deeper problem than just you being annoyed by a child. Many times, there is a problem present that is not understood or recognized; therefore, it goes untreated.

- **Physical and mental ailments** — A lot of child care centers accept children when they are infants and toddlers. As that child grows, they may develop certain problems that you can no longer provide for. For instance, Robert began coming to your in home child care center when he was eight weeks old. As he grew, his development seemed a little off compared to the other children, but he was still growing and doing well in other areas. However, the older he got, the more pronounced the problems became. His parents also recognized the problems, and he was taken for diagnosis. The tests came back positive that he was autistic. The parents consulted you, and you began some specialized activities for him each day. The activities took away from your time with the other children, and as Robert grew, he demanded even more time. His needs were overshadowing the needs of the other children, but it was not possible for you to hire an assistant just to provide adequate care for Robert. Therefore, Robert had to leave and find a center that could pay special attention to his needs.

Letting Robert go may have been extra hard because you still cared about him and his family, but knew his needs were beyond what you could provide for. Most families will understand this, and be sympathetic to your business needs, too. Just in case they are not, document the problems you encounter on your journey to providing the adequate care.

"*Children are like wet cement. Whatever falls on*
them makes an impression."
Dr. Haim Ginott

13

FOOD & BEVERAGE MANAGEMENT

The children in your care have many needs: a nurturing environment, toys, developmentally appropriate activities, and most of all – food. In your child care center, you have two options: to provide food and beverages or not. We discussed the pros and cons of food service earlier, but now we will delve into managing food and beverages for the children. You will need careful planning to have the adequate number of supplies on hand to supply the daily and weekly needs for everyone.

The food you serve will be based on the hours you are open. When you are open early morning, you can serve breakfast to the children as standard fare or you can make it an optional plan with a set fee. Not every family needs to have early morning care and some prefer to have breakfast with their children at home. If breakfast will be included in their normal fee, ask them to provide a schedule of when they will be having breakfast so you make enough for everyone.

BREAKFAST

To keep breakfast running smoothly, set a time when it will be served. When a child is not there within 15 or 20 minutes of the serving time, they forfeit breakfast. It would be impossible, especially in a large center, to keep feeding children as they come in at all different times. Make it known what time breakfast is served, so that the parents will know and can plan at home.

Planning a menu will also keep the hectic morning hour more manageable. Schedule a week's worth of menu offerings, so before the children arrive you can prepare the ingredients or get the plates, silverware, and bowls ready. The more you can have prepared ahead of time will make it smoother when there are 3, 6, 12, or 20 hungry children wanting food now. Items that can be made easily ahead of time, and warmed up at the allotted breakfast time, are pancakes, waffles, French toast sticks, and hash browns. Cereal can be made quickly. Items that may take a little more time to prepare are eggs, sausage, oatmeal, and pastries.

BREAKFAST MENU		
Monday	Tuesday	Wednesday
Pancakes	Oatmeal	Dry Cereal
Syrup	Vanilla yogurt with blueberries	Milk
Apple Juice		Orange Juice
	Toast with jelly	Bananas
Thursday		Friday
French toast sticks		Scrambled eggs
Syrup		Sausage links
Strawberries		Hash browns
Grape juice		Apple Juice

If you want to keep the routine the same, use this menu every week. If you are a large enough center with a cook, you can use more and fancier recipes. When you use the same menu week after week, you know exactly how many supplies you will need for the upcoming week. You can scan the pantry, check the level in the pancake mix, for example, and replenish it if needed. Fresh fruit will need to be purchased weekly, as does the yogurt.

Alternate the variety of fruit juices you offer in the morning. To be eligible for food program reimbursement, the juice will need to be 100 juice and not a partial blend. Milk is also suitable for serving at all meals or snack time.

MORNING SNACK

A morning snack is another option. Before you offer a morning snack, you might want to take into account your day. If some children arrive later, they might not be hungry around 10 a.m. when a snack would be served. However, if you wait until later, the snack may get in the way of lunchtime. Then the children will not each lunch, and it will be an ugly cycle throughout the day. A morning snack may be dependant upon the day – and you can decide from one day to the next if one will be needed. If you have a particularly active morning, offer a light snack. The children may surprise you and not be hungry anyway.

Morning Snack Options:

- Apple slices

- Bananas slices with peanut butter

- Crackers with cheese

• Grapes

• Carrot sticks with dip

• Pear slices

• Peach slices

• Raisins

Lunch Time

The prime food management will come with lunch time. If you belong to the food program, you will need to pick foods under their guidelines. With lunch, you will need to have a serving of fruit and a serving of vegetables. At an in home center with fewer mouths to feed, finding something that everyone likes may be a little easier. It may be difficult to please everyone in a large center, so planning a menu and sticking to it will be the best plan of action.

LUNCH MENU		
Monday	Tuesday	Wednesday
Peanut butter and jelly sandwiches	Homemade macaroni and cheese	Homemade pizza
Apple slices	Green beans	Peaches
Carrot sticks	Fruit cocktail	Pudding
Ranch dressing	Milk	Milk
Milk	Jell-o	

LUNCH MENU		
Thursday		Friday
Hamburgers and bun		Spaghetti
Cheese		Sauce
Applesauce		Corn
Peas		Breadsticks
Milk		Pineapple
		Milk

This is just a basic menu of foods that most children eat. If you have children with special needs or allergies, you may need to be much more creative. In a home child care center, the food variety will be easier to manage. When there are not as many mouths to feed, you can make dishes that take longer to prepare. You can also be more selective since you do not need to make huge batches to give every one a large enough portion.

To shop or order food for a large group, plan out at least two weeks worth of menus at one time. Make a list of perishables you can buy ahead of time and store them. Then, make a list of fresh foods and milk that will need to be purchased only a few days ahead of time. When you know exactly what you need and how much, it will make the shopping quicker and less expensive if you do not overbuy by accident.

The best bet would be to make an inventory checklist and keep a set number of items in stock at all times. At the end of each week, take inventory of what is left over. Then cross check that with your list, and you know what you will need to shop for. For instance, one in home child care provider in Michigan gives her children milk during lunch and their snack. She knows they will go through two gallons of milk each week. On Sunday night, she buys two gallons of milk and knows she will be adequately stocked for the entire week.

In home and small centers will need to juggle a little during preparation time. Often times, the sole caregiver is the cook. Only in the big centers do you have the luxury of hiring a separate cook. When you are the sole caregiver but need to prepare food, pick an activity that will keep the children entertained for a long period of time. This may be the time to put in a short video or have a cartoon running. Some children will even sit long enough to color several pages or read a book by themselves. Whatever works best for your group of children is key.

Afternoon Snack

Having an afternoon snack available for the children will be more important than having a morning snack. After nap time, the children will sometimes have two, three, or even more hours until they have dinner. Make the afternoon snack healthy, but not so filling that they will not want to eat any dinner.

Afternoon snack ideas:

- Graham crackers and cream cheese

- Crackers and peanut butter

- Celery and peanut butter

- Apples with peanut butter

- Cheese and crackers

- Animal crackers

- Bananas

- Homemade cookies

Milk and juice can be served with the afternoon snack as well. Chocolate milk may be a treat for your children, too, if the state has approved it within their food program guidelines.

Some days are special and require an appropriate snack. Children might bring a treat in for their birthday party. Cupcakes, cakes, and cookies will probably be the normal fare. On holidays, you can also have a grand celebration with treats. When you do have a lot of treats come in for a party, try and balance it and have healthy snacks brought in, too.

WHERE TO BUY YOUR FOOD

Having children in your care will require many groceries. The best place to do your shopping is at a store that sells bulk quantities for a discount or a food supplier. You will have to determine the best provider is for you. Not only will shopping at a discount store take time, you will have to load it, unload it, and store it right after you buy it. A food distributor will load it at their warehouse, drive it to you, and unload it in your kitchen.

While food suppliers may not be an option for the small provider, you may be surprised. Shop around in your area and inquire about prices for their food and service. And another place to check is your favorite grocery store. More and more people are requesting delivery service, so you may be able to benefit, too. You can place an order of food online or over the phone; the store will have a shopper gather your items and deliver them to your house for an additional fee on top of the groceries.

A large food supplier will have a list of food they can supply you with at a discounted price. If you belong to a franchise, you may get a deeper discount if all the centers use their service. With a large food supplier, you can have a standing order and not have to worry about ordering the correct food week to week or making out a new list to go shopping each week.

The Pros of Using a Food Supplier

- **Convenience** — The food is brought to your door.

- **Availability of discounts** — Buying in bulk or large quantities or being part of a franchise can earn you significant discounts on food.

- **Standing orders** — If there is a standing order in place, it will save you from having to check your inventory every week. It will also save you from making a list and doing the shopping.

The Cons of Using a Food Supplier

- **Some food is heavily processed and ready made.** With the convenience of prepared foods, the health quality can go down. Typically, prepared and canned foods are higher in sodium content and less in vitamin content than foods that are made from scratch.

- **Limited selection** — Although having a standing order is convenient, your order may be on a limited selection of foods. If you have dietary restrictions, you may need to go to the supermarket to provide for that child, erasing your convenience factor.

You will need to determine which the right method is for you and your home or facility. Generally, home providers just add to their weekly shopping and have the center's groceries put on separate receipts when checking out.

SPECIALTY FOODS

A food supplier will not be able to supply all the food items you require. When there are infants and toddlers in your care, you will have to decide if you will provide the formula and milk for them. In small and in home centers, the parents usually provide their specific brand of formula for their baby. In large centers, you have the option of parents bringing in their own or supplying them with a generic brand that your center can receive at a discount. There are child care supply stores that offer formula, diapers, and wipes at a discount to large child care centers. When the child care center can provide the formula, it is a little less of an expense for the parent since they do not need to keep a supply at home and at their care center.

In addition to needing formula, growing babies should have whole milk to help their development. Studies have shown that babies need to have the full fat in milk in order for their brain cells to develop. Their bodies are able to eat and digest the whole milk, even with its high fat and cholesterol content, with no ill effects. Children do not need to worry about the calories and fat content in milk until they are six years or older. The longer they drink whole milk, the more brain cell development they may get.

As a baby grows, they will need to begin baby food. This is another food you will have to check in to the feasibility of providing it versus having the parents provide it. Some supply stores will provide jars of generic baby food, but it will still add up quickly. To make things more convenient for your families, you may consider adding a surcharge onto infants until they are eating solid foods if the parent does not want to bring their jars every day.

STORING FOOD

When you purchase your food supplies, it should be stored in its own shelving system or pantry. All food in non-perishable containers, such as cans or boxes, must be placed on shelves that are separate from shelving units that may contain cleaning products, soap, or even paper goods. This prevents any contamination, even though the cans and jars are sealed, from occurring in your home.

Feeding the Staff

You will need to determine if food is a benefit of working at your child care center. The employees will all need to eat lunch, too, when you have a big center. You will need to decide if you can feed everyone within your budget and still have enough to feed the children. When you do provide the food for the adults in you employ, you may want to have them sign up each morning if they will be eating lunch that day. That way you can have enough food prepared and made for everyone. If you do not provide food for employees, they can bring their own lunch or go out to eat.

There will need to be guidelines to prevent the abuse of food provided to the employees. When you own and operate a large center, you may need to place locks on cupboards, pantries, or shelving to keep containers and supplies from mysteriously leaving. You would be surprised to find out what goes on when the owner is away.

One large center in eastern Pennsylvania had a problem with large pudding containers being taken from the kitchen. The cook knew she had purchased enough for the children to eat on a particular day, but when it came time to open the large cans, she was one short. This happened several times during a two month period. A memo was sent to all the employees asking what had happened to the pudding. No one knew anything, of course, and the pudding mystery was not solved for several more weeks. It turns out, one of the college aged helpers, who was low on funds, thought the pudding would not be missed and routinely swiped a can to keep in her dorm room for her and her roommate.

Cleaning the Pantry

Not only is ordering and shopping for food important to your child care center, so is cleaning out the food. When you run a large center, you may be surprised at how fast the refrigerator fills up, even though you purchased the industrial sized model. The staff will need to place their lunches and such in the refrigerator, the infant room will have bottles and formula that need to be kept cold, and the next thing you know, there is not any room in the fridge for your food.

The best way to manage food supplies is with a marker. Make it a rule that anything brought in to the kitchen, whether it is stored in the refrigerator or on a shelf, has the date it entered written on it in ink. That way, when the forgotten dish of vegetable dip is discovered at the back of the fridge, all you have to do is see the date which is three months past and know to throw it away. The same can work for any non-perishable foods you purchase. Simply writing the date on the can will make it easier for you to know how close the foods are to being used up.

Another way to manage food in the kitchen is by having a monthly clean out date. Post a sign on the fridge or in the kitchen and tell everyone who uses the fridge that if something is in the fridge, it must have a name and current date on it or it will be tossed. Old food in the refrigerator can be just as unsafe as dairy products or meat left on the counter for days on end. Food only lasts a few days in the fridge, unless it is a condiment in a sealed can.

CASE STUDY: P. NICKY FOSTER

I found the easiest part of opening the business was setting up the actual equipment in the classrooms. I had a vision of what I wanted to see in a child care facility based on my experience as a working mom with children in child care. There were certain things I wanted so that I could make the center feel more like home than an institution. So I incorporated things like mood lighting, music

CASE STUDY: P. NICKY FOSTER

for naptime, sheets and blankets on the cots, curtains in the infant room, and good food.

The hardest part for me was that I started the business without any loans from a bank. My husband and I took our life savings, including our retirement plan funds and a few loans from our family, to get started. Over time this was good for keeping our expenses down. However, when our reserves got really low and our cash flow was terrible, the banks would not loan us any money. I would suggest that people interested in the business get bank loans first and use their savings or reserves to help the business stay afloat.

A tip I always tell new entrepreneurs is to find out who their licensing specialists are and develop a relationship with them. Tap into their knowledge of licensing rules and guidelines to help you figure out how to maintain the rules in your state. Also, do not be afraid to contact them when you have a problem and you need advice. Always be honest with them no matter what.

Before I got started, I wish I had known more about how to find a quality curriculum. It took a while before I found one that was comprehensive and one that was easy for the teachers to use.

Always pay close attention to the developments in the state legislature regarding changes in the child care industry. Laws heavily influence sustainability and operations. You may have the opportunity to help steer those changes if you become involved in the legislative process. Find professional organizations in your area that can keep you involved in the industry and that can help you make professional connections.

Stay away from long-term leases if possible. After operating for a while you might find that buying your real estate is more cost effective

CASE STUDY: P. NICKY FOSTER

than leasing. Long-term leases keep you trapped in an arrangement in which the owner may not want to sell and would rather raise the rent annually.

If you are going into business, make sure you have proper professionals to help you with the organization of the company. Get good lawyers to help create your company. Get good accountants who can help you keep your profits. Get a good payroll company to ensure that your taxes and tax reports are done in a timely fashion. These professionals help lift these burdens so you can concentrate on running your business.

My best experience as a day care provider is usually preschool graduation; it is a happy time for me. Some of the children that graduate have made their way from infant rooms to preschool graduation, and to see them grow and develop is just a magnificent source of pride and pleasure for me. I keep in touch through kindergarten just to see how they are doing academically. All our children leave our academy ready to learn.

I previously thought that getting out of the corporate setting would allow me to work less. I find that I work and worry more because I am ultimately responsible for the success or lack thereof in this organization. I did not think I could be this self-motivated. Yet everyday I am looking for ways to take our center to a higher level of service and to stomp out the competition.

"He who teaches children learns more than they do"

~ German Proverb

14
EMERGENCY POLICIES

Even though it is great to have a positive outlook in life, you need to be prepared for the worst. An accident can occur with no notice at all; however, you need to be prepared to react without hesitation. These accidents can come in the form of a weather emergency, a fire, a homeland security issue, or a medical incident. A quick, efficient response is best to keep everyone calm and to deal with the situation effectively.

CRISIS MANAGEMENT

You should have a basic crisis management plan in place for any type of emergency. This crisis plan will detail who to contact, what to do, how to handle the children, and so forth. Careful training for your staff members will ensure that when and if a real crisis were to occur, it would be handled efficiently and effectively.

The crisis emergency plan should list the chain of command. That way, if you had a large or medium sized center, and you were away at the time, the working staff would immediately go to the list and see who the next person is in the chain of command.

The crisis management should also list the duties of the first in command. Do they alert a person off site of the crisis? Do emergency medical personnel need to be on stand-by? Should the media be alerted to a potentially dangerous situation? Should parents be called to come and get their children? These scenarios should be discussed in depth in a separate emergency plan, such as fire, weather disasters, security threats, and health emergencies.

In case of crisis and emergencies, a basic kit of supplies should be prepared. This kit should be stored in a sealed rubber container that can be easily grabbed by you or a staff member.

This kit should include:

- First aid supplies
- Drinking water
- Emergency contact information for all children and staff members (in a sealed bag to prevent water damage)
- Flashlight
- Batteries for flashlights and radios
- Radio
- Non-perishable food in cans

Depending on how large your center is, having non-perishable food items may be very difficult. However, you can keep enough canned goods stocked in your kitchen for several days. If the emergency were a snowstorm, you would be able to use the building and have access to the kitchen. When the crisis is more severe, say a train derailed nearby and you had to seal yourself in a room in the building, you would not be able to leave the safe room and get more food.

Another tricky part to planning for a disaster is if you have infants and babies. They will require diapers, formula, or breast milk. Breast milk would be impossible if the mother was not around. However, a can of formula and a package of diapers can easily be stored in the rubber container. A package of wipes and an extra blanket may also be a good idea for your disaster kit.

FIRE EMERGENCIES

Fire drills should be practiced once a month to keep the children aware of what should happen if the smoke detector or fire alarm ever rings for real. Since a fire can happen at any time during any month, the drills should be practiced as though they were life-like. The children may have to go outside when it is chilly or raining if a fire were to break out. Fires do not always happen on warm, sunny days and neither should fire drills.

The fire drill is most effective if it is random. Staff members who know ahead of time are not necessarily on their toes because they had preparation time. They need to be trained on what to grab and how to act without any preparation time.

A map with the house or building layout should be placed in each room where the children are. In large centers, a map is in every room to show the exit door and the route used to get to that door. The route should be drawn in with arrows or colored marker to clearly show which way to go.

Near the exit door or classroom door, there should be an emergency folder and first aid kit. Both should be grabbed and taken outside with the children. See below for the contents of the first aid kit and emergency folder.

If a fire were to break out in your center, the children and staff should know what to do since they have been practicing their fire drills. In reality, a fire drill is much less scary to practice than when real smoke is pouring down the halls. Since the smoke is dark and makes it hard to breathe and see through, it is vital to react quickly. Get yourself to safety and call 911 as soon as possible.

When a fire alarm or smoke detector goes off, immediately gather the children if they are small and carry them outside. If you have a fenced perimeter, go to the spot that is as far away from the structure as possible. When there is no fence, choose a safe spot and wait for the authorities to arrive.

If the fire occurs in a large center, a provider designated ahead of time will always be in charge of that room. The children should line up behind the exit door of the room and follow the adult in charge outside. Once outside, the adult who is in charge should use their emergency folder list, take role call, and account for children. Once the children are accounted for, make sure there are no minor injuries that require attention. Reassurance will be needed by many frightened children.

You, being the owner or director of the center, need to maintain your own folder for emergencies. Your folder will contain a list of every adult who is in charge of each room. Your job is to go to each teacher and check that they have accounted for every child outside of the building. Your emergency folder should also have copies of every child's contact information, as well as the contact information for every employee.

When practicing your fire drills, you also have a few extra steps to remember as a caregiver. When a fire alarm goes off, you should be trained to grab a first aid kit and an emergency folder. The first aid kit will have the basic supplies to treat any cuts or bruises that happen when getting away from the house or building. Inside your emergency folder should be a roster of the children. If you own a large center, each teacher should have a folder in their emergency kit with a list of children in their classroom. On each roster should be the contact information for each child's parents. When it is safe to make phone call or if you have a cell phone, begin calling parents to alert them their child is safe and to come and get them.

FIRST AID KIT CONTENTS

- Band-aids
- Gauze
- Ace bandages
- Antibiotic ointment
- Tweezers
- Children's Tylenol

You can also purchase a ready-made first aid kit at any drug store, grocery store, or department store. They are available in different sizes to accommodate the size of the child care center you run.

EMERGENCY FOLDER CONTENTS

- Up to date roster (for each class if a center)
- Contact information for each child
- Medical information for each child
- Emergency contacts for a center if you are not available
- A checklist of protocol if you have franchise rules to follow

A fire can do a lot of damage quickly. Water can do even more damage than smoke and fire, in some cases. If there is damage to your house or center, you may need to prepare the families to find alternate care for a few days until you can have the center cleaned up. When significant damage occurs, you will have to evaluate the situation, maybe even with an insurance agent, to get the true estimate of damages and restoration time. You may need to consider an alternate location to provide care for some of the children if you have a large center.

Tornado

A tornado is a real concern in areas of the United States and Canada. Most places will not need to worry about tornado drills or preparedness, but in the Midwest and southern areas, you will need to conduct tornado drills.

Planning for a tornado is similar to planning for a fire – you cannot. They can occur with very little or no warning at any time of the year. Their suddenness is what can cause the most damage. Proper tornado drills for the children, and the caregivers if you have a large center, will prepare everyone ahead of time so they know how to handle one if it does happen.

A tornado escape drill will also require a written plan like a fire escape does. For large centers, there should be a map of the building in each room displayed prominently. The map in each room shows the specific location where those children and adults should retreat to if a tornado warning is issued.

A basement would be the safest place for anyone to wait out a tornado warning. Home child care centers will usually have a basement in the house. Sometimes the main operation of a home child care center is in the basement, so no extra precautions are required. A basement for a large center is not usually feasible, just because of the size and cost factor when building.

When there is no basement in the child care facility, a bathroom or hallway without windows is the next best choice. The interior walls are the safest and usually have no windows, so they are the first choice. If there is no interior wall without windows nearby, use it anyway and have a blanket or something protective to wrap over you. The wrap will shield you from glass flying and small cuts to the skin.

When a tornado warning is issued, most communities sound a siren. When the siren is heard, even if it is the monthly practice for the system, practice your tornado drill.

When the siren is heard, take the children to the basement or interior wall. In a home child care center, keep them close together. In a large center, the children will need to line up at the door and file into the designated safe spot for that room. Since big centers have a lot of children, it may become crowded.

The proper position for the children to be in is facing the wall and on their knees. If they are kneeling, it takes up less room, and you can crowd more children in together. Each child needs to take their hands and place them over the back of the neck, covering their head. This is supposed to protect their neck and head from injury. Remind them to keep quiet and urge them to stay calm.

Tornado warnings can last anywhere from minutes to hours. If the tornado warning does not seem to be an imminent threat, you could read books or sing quietly to keep the kids entertained while remaining in the safe spot.

Once the tornado warning has passed or been cancelled, the children can file back into their room or you can head out of the basement. In the case of a tornado drill, keep the children in place for five to ten minutes so they will know what to do quickly in the event of a real tornado.

LOCAL SECURITY

Several other situations may arise that involve security on a local level. More and more, we are seeing hostage situations in houses, schools, or places of business. To keep yourself and the children safe, you should employ a policy on how to handle, or even prevent, a breach in security.

A breach in your security can come in the form of a stranger entering your house or child care center. They may think there is money on the premise and simply want to take it and flee. Another stranger may see it as a way to get attention by holding hostages and getting ransom demands met. Both scenarios can be very dangerous and should be handled with the utmost care.

The safety of everyone is the top priority. If possible, give the intruder what they want so they leave quickly. Call 911 immediately after they are gone and lock the doors. Write down any description you can remember to help the police track down the intruder.

If a burglary is not their intent, it is hard to predict what to do. Inform the children to remain calm and quiet and try to reason with the intruder. Call the authorities by any means possible, whether it is a cell phone or panic button on a security system.

Sometimes a breach in security will come in the form of a parent. Divorces are very common these days, and chances are you will have several children from split families in your care. Not all divorces are amicable, nor do they result in joint custody. If there is a child in your care that is the sole custody of one parent, you need to keep records of it. The custodial parent needs to document that the child is not to be released to the other parent under any conditions. This may also hold true for grandparents.

If a parent or grandparent comes to pick up the child and they are not authorized by the custodial parent, you do not release the child. Contact the custodial parent immediately and alert them to the situation. If the parent or grandparent is not cooperative, call the authorities. There is a reason why the child(ren) cannot be with the other parent, and you are upholding the custodial parent's directions.

Conversely, if the custodial parent simply does not want to have the other parent pick the child(ren) up, but there is no written judgment preventing the other parent from doing so, you cannot legally hold the child. It must be in writing who is and who is not authorized to pick up a child.

If the situation becomes tense, or escalated, follow the routine as if it were a stranger intruder. Contact the authorities as soon as possible and protect the children. Keep them calm and quiet and reassure them that everything will be all right.

NATIONAL SECURITY (TERRORISM)

Since 9/11, the world is a very different place in which to live and operate a business. No longer can you trust anyone off of the street, let alone from a different city or state. The federal government created a homeland security organization to provide security for national affairs and to help people prepare themselves and be alert to any forms of terrorism. One way they urge people to be prepared is with a plan. You should have a plan to follow in the case of a national security breach and educate your staff and families about it.

A plan to follow after a national security issue can be simple or involved. Some of the plan will be tailor made to where you live. If you reside in a large city, your chances of an attack are the same as any other location, but the complexities come in with the population. A large city has many more people to alert, many more transportation routes to cover, and many more avenues for destruction and confusion.

For example, if a bomb were to land in Miami, a lot of damage could be done to buildings, roads, and communication tools. But since Miami has a high population, they also have more roads, buildings, and communication tools to use as alternatives. Your plan should detail all the alternatives you plan to use in case the normal ones you follow are knocked out.

Some examples of what to include in your national security threat plan:

- Emergency contact numbers for you or your center should the main phone line go down.

- What alternative location you would take the children to if needed.

- What procedure needs to be followed in order for someone other than a parent to pick up a child.

- What radio stations or TV channels you would send a message to if you could.

- How you would care for the child if and when an emergency would occur.

Accidents seem to be a large part of a child's existence — a scraped knee here, a bruised elbow there. The majority of children's injuries are minor and will only require minor first aid, if any. You do need to be prepared on how to handle a major medical emergency, because on occasion, they do happen.

An emergency medical situation may be an allergic reaction, a cut that requires stitches, or a fall with a possible broken bone. The severity of the injury determines what you do first. A serious injury where there is heavy bleeding, unconsciousness, or breathing difficulties needs to be handled by professionals. Contact 911 immediately. Keep the child, or staff member, calm and as comfortable as possible until help arrives.

When smaller incidents occur like cuts that may need stitches or a fall that might involve a broken bone, call the parents immediately. The injury is not life threatening, but requires prompt attention. If the parents' work location is far away or they cannot gauge how serious the injury is, give them the option of calling 911. That way the child can get the attention quickly while the parent is en route to the hospital. In the meantime, keep the child as comfortable as possible until the parents or paramedics arrive to take them to the doctor or emergency room.

For minor injuries, like cuts, scrapes, and bruises, clean the wound carefully with soap and water. Apply a bandage or dressing as necessary to keep it clean and to stop the bleeding. Antibacterial ointment can be applied under bandages to keep the germs away.

With any injury, large or small, it needs to be documented. A form for all medical mishaps should be filled out with copies given to the parents and one kept for the center. On the form should be the names of all children and staff members involved. There should be a summary of the accident and how it happened. Any treatment given should also be documented and kept in a file for several years.

The documentation can protect you or your business if a family ever decides to sue. If you have documentation, you can refute any bogus claims. You can also easily keep track of exactly what happened and who was involved.

See the resources section for a sample incident report sheet.

There are many other situations that need a specific plan of action. Some of them may include:

- Planning for a train derailment if you live near a railroad track.
- A hurricane plan if you are near the ocean.
- A backup location if you live in an area prone to blackouts.
- A lockdown plan if you live near a prison.
- An emergency route if you live in a flash flood zone.

The list could go on and on since there are so many things that happen in our lives. Have a plan for any and every type of disaster that may strike.

CASE STUDY: KIM M. VUKELJA

I loved being a mom and I loved my child but, I needed something more. I needed to return to the work force, but shopping around for child care proved to be an extremely depressing task. I could not find a facility that I felt was appropriate for my little girl. I wanted a safe, clean, warm environment.

I wanted an educational program that would be stimulating, challenging, and developmentally appropriate.

"I can do better than the daycares that I am finding out there," I told my husband.

Instead of going back to work as a counselor at the local mental health agency I decided to open my own pre-school.

Finding a site, getting a license, and choosing a curriculum were the easy tasks in getting started. A real estate agent helped locate a building for me to purchase. The state had specific regulations and paperwork that were necessary to get the license. I did a bit of research to find a developmentally appropriate curriculum. I was ready to open my doors, or so I thought.

I started to interview potential teachers, which proved to be the biggest challenge of all.

Finding a team of dedicated professionals who have the patience and compassion to deal with pre-school age children was very difficult. I found myself asking, "Would I want this person to work with my own child?" This was the litmus test, and it was the best way to judge an applicant. I still use this question as my guide when looking for potential employees.

CASE STUDY: KIM M. VUKELJA

Another important question to ask is, "What skills do you have that you can use to positively influence young children?" Over the years I have learned that training a person to fit into our program using their own personal skills gives the teacher a sense of satisfaction, while at the same time benefiting the program. If you find a person that has the values you desire in an employee/teacher work with them, train them, and empower them to be the best they can be.

I look forward to working with the staff, the parents, and, most of all, the children. I am active in many community events for children; I stay on top of current changes in the childcare industry, and keep the school current with any new requirements. An owner can not do it alone; the staff makes the school. A quality program requires a qualified staff and a dedicated leader. Being actively involved as a "hands-on" director is what I feel has made the biggest difference in the success of my pre-school.

The alarm loudly awakens me five mornings a week and I get out of bed and head to the pre-school. I have raised five children, taken them to work with me, and after 25 years I still am excited about my program. I feel that this profession is a perfect job for a mother.

Imagination Station is a Gold Seal School in Florida and has been accredited by the National Accreditation Commission for Early Care and Education Programs. For more information, contact the school using the following information:

Imagination Station Montessori
528 N. Peninsula Dr.
Daytona Beach, FL 32118
386-255-3755
imaginationstn@bellsouth.net

"Children will not remember you for the material things you provided but for the feeling that you cherished them."

~ Richard L. Evans

15
GOING FORWARD

As your business grows, your needs may change. You will have to adapt old policy to fit your current needs if it does not already do so. Every few years, evaluate your practices and policies and make sure they are current and working for you. Read over your mission statement and see if you are following it. Whenever something you created at the beginning of your child care operation does not fit with what you are doing, update it. Several avenues of your business will need updating often.

RATE INCREASES

When a year or two has passed since your opening, you will need to re-evaluate your rates. Are they still sufficient? Do they cover all the expenses or is it time to increase the rate?

When you are increasing the rate, consider doing it several ways. First, make it enough so that you will not have to do it again any time soon. Parents seem to balk less at one $10 hike every four years rather than a $2.50 hike each year. If the rate only jumps once every few years, they can say, "Oh, it's not so bad. It was several years ago the last time she raised her rates."

Put It in Writing

Write a letter and give it to each family detailing the rate increase. If the increase is high, you may want to provide a list of reasons to justify the jump. If the reasons are spelled out and they can see the benefits their child will receive, they may offer no complaints. Post the letter at the entry to your house or center, where it will be displayed and noticed. This will act as a reminder and they will have no excuse that they did not know. The week before the families will be making the increased payments, make notes. Use red marker and underline the letter – "This is next week!" Do not be pushy about it, just straightforward.

Give Ample Notice

When you do raise your rates, give ample notice. Do not expect to send out a letter on Friday and be paid the extra amount on Monday. Families might need to work on their budgets or make some adjustments to accommodate your fees. Six weeks is adequate time to notify the families of the rate change. If a family cannot afford or does not agree with your rate increase, they will have enough time to search for a new provider and give you two week's notice of their intentions, before the increase takes place.

HEALTH POLICIES

As the world grows, we are becoming more and more exposed to diseases. Some concerns that have emerged recently involve the flu and unusual strains. When and if these strains affect a larger portion of the population, you may need to re-evaluate your health policy. With the government predicting gloom and doom, you never know what to expect if bird flu does become a major human health risk. You may need to restrict anyone from your care if they show symptoms of flu. That will have to be considered when the time comes; just be aware.

TRAINING

Training for you and any staff you may have will change almost every year. How many classes you need to attend, what classes you have to have before opening, and licensing requirements are always changing. It is not to say it is bad; officials are just trying to improve the conditions for everyone and to streamline regulations regarding children and their care. Training classes may be required to handle any health developments in the future. They may also require everyone to have six, eight, or more CEUs during one year.

LICENSING

When your license is nearing renewal time, check with your licensing agency to find out if there are any changes are so you can begin implementing them. If you begin the process early, making the changes will not be so drastic. The sooner you get used to following them, the easier it will be for everyone. And remember that the changes are made with your best interests in mind. The licensing requirements are made to keep people out of the business, but make those in the business have a more enjoyable, rewarding experience.

"There is a garden in every childhood, an enchanted place where colors are brighter, the air softer, and the morning more fragrant than ever again."

~ Elizabeth Lawrence

CONCLUSION

I hope this book will give you a head start on preparing to open and operate your own child care center. It may seem like a ton of information and overwhelming at first, but with a little guidance, you can be a pro in no time at all. If you still need a little guidance, call someone in your area and ask them questions specific to your region. What better way to get the answers than by someone who is in the trenches?

Use this book as a guide, take notes, write in the margins, and have fun during the process. After all, you want to work with children or you would not even have read this book. Opening a child care is an excellent way to fulfill your dreams and your financial goals. Good luck on your journey.

"Life loves to be taken by the lapel and told:

"I'm with you kid. Let's go."

~ Maya Angelou

APPENDIX A

STATE ASSOCIATIONS

Each child care center is regulated by the state in which it is located. Below is the agency to contact for more information on licensing and regulations in your state. If they do not have the adequate paperwork to begin the licensing process, they can direct you to who does. Allow several weeks or even months for the licensing process to be completed.

Alabama
Department of Human Resources
Office of Day Care
50 N. Ripley
Montgomery, AL 36130
334-242-1425
http://www.dhr.state.al.us/page.asp?pageid=255

Alaska
Department of Health and Social Services
Division of Public Assistance Child Care Programs Office
619 E. Ship Creek Ave., Suite #230
Anchorage, AK 99567
907-269-4600
http://www.hss.state.ak.us/dpa/programs/ccare/regs.html

Arizona

Division of Licensing Services
Office of Child Care Licensing
150 N. 18th Avenue, Suite #400
Phoenix, AZ 85007-3224
602-364-2536 (within AZ) or 800-615-8555
http://www.azdhs.gov/als/childcare/

Arkansas

Division of Childcare and Early Childhood Education
Child Care Licensing
P.O. Box 1437, Slot S150
Little Rock, AR 72203-1437
501-682-8590 or 800-445-3316
http://www.state.ar.us/childcare/provinfo.html

California

California Department of Social Services
Community Care Licensing Division
Child Care Program Office
744 P Street, M.S. 19-48
Sacramento, CA 95814
http://www.ccld.ca.gov/res/pdf/CClistingMaster.pdf
http://www.ccld.ca.gov
http://www.buildingchildcare.org/

Colorado

Division of Child Care
Colorado Department of Human Services
1575 Sherman Street
Denver, CO 80203-1714
800-799-5876 or 303-866-5958
http://www.cdhs.state.co.us/childcare/licensing.htm

Connecticut

State of Connecticut
Department of Public Health
410 Capital Avenue MS #12 DAC
P.O. Box 340308
Hartford, CT 06134-0308
860-509-8045
http://www.dph.state.ct.us/BRS/Day_Care/day_care.htm

Delaware

Office of Child Care Licensing
1825 Faulkland Road
Wilmington, DE 19805
302-892-5800 or 800-822-2236
http://www.state.de.us/kids/occl/occl_resources.shtml

District of Columbia

District of Columbia Department of Health
Health Care Regulation and Licensing Office
Child and Residential Care Facilities Division
Child Care Licensing Branch
825 N. Capitol Street, N.E., 2nd Floor
Washington, D.C., 20002
202-442-5888
**http://doh.dc.gov/doh/frames.asp?doc=/doh/lib/doh/pdf/29_dcmr_chapter3
regulations.pdf&group=1787&open=|33120|33139|**

Florida

Florida Department of Children and Families
Child Care Services
1317 Winewood Blvd.,
Building 6, Room 389-A
Tallahassee, FL 32399-0700
850-488-4900
http://www.myflorida.com/childcare/

Georgia

Bright From the Start
GA Department of Early Care and Learning
10 Park Place South, Suite #600
Atlanta, GA 30303
404-657-5562 or (888) 442-7735
http://www.decal.state.ga.us

Hawaii

Department of Human Services
Benefit, Employment, and Support Services Division
Employment/Child Care Program Office
820 Mililani St, Suite 606
Haseko Center
Honolulu, HI 96813
808-586-7058
**http://www.hawaii.gov/dhs/main/har/har_current/AdminRules/
document_view**

Idaho

Department of Health & Welfare
Bureau of Family and Children Services
5th Floor
P.O. Box 83720
Boise, ID 83720-0036
208-334-5689 or 800-926-2588 (Contact the following cities for their
specific licensing
rules: Boise, Coeur d'Alene, Lewiston, Malta, Pocatello)
http://adm.idaho.gov/adminrules/rules/idapa16/16index.htm

Illinois

State of Illinois
Department of Children & Family Services
406 East Monroe Street
Springfield, IL 62701-1498
217-524-1983 or 877-746-0829
http://www.state.il.us/dcfs/policy/pr_policy_rules.shtml

Indiana

Family and Social Services Administration
Division of Family Resources
402 W. Washington St. Room W386
Indianapolis, IN 46204
877-511-1144
http://www.in.gov/fssa/carefinder/

Iowa

Child Care Unit
Iowa Department of Human Services
Division of BDP-FAC
Hoover State Office Building
Des Moines, IA 50319-0114
515-281-5657
http://www.dhs.state.ia.us/policyanalysis/RulesPages/RulesChap.htm

Kansas

Kansas Department of Health & Environment
Bureau of Child Care and Health Facilities
Child Care Licensing & Registration Section
900 SW Jackson Street, Suite 200
Topeka, KS 66612-1274
785-296-1270
http://www.kdhe.state.ks.us/bcclr/index.html

Kentucky

Division of Child Care
Cabinet for Families and Children
275 East Main Street
Frankfort, KY 40621
502-564-2524 for family homes; (502) 564-2800 for centers
http://www.lrc.state.ky.us/kar/TITLE922.HTM

Louisiana

Department of Social Services
Bureau of Licensing
P.O. Box 3078
Baton Rouge, LA 70821
225-922-0015
http://www.dss.state.la.us/departments/os/Licensing_.html

Maine

Maine Department of Human Services
Division of Licensing
Child Care Licensing Unit.
State House Station 11
221 State Street
Augusta, ME 04333-0011
207-287-5060
http://www.maine.gov/dhhs/occhs/cclicensing.htm

Maryland

State Department of Education
Office of Child Care
200 W. Baltimore Street
Baltimore, MD 21201
410-767-7805 or (800) 332-6347
http://www.marylandpublicschools.org/msde/divisions/child_care/

Massachusetts

Department of Early Education and Care
51 Sleeper St, 4th Floor
Boston, MA 02210
617-988-6600
http://www.eec.state.ma.us/

Michigan

Division of Child Day Care Licensing
Michigan Department of Human Services
7109 W. Saginaw, 2nd Floor
P.O. Box 30650
Lansing, MI 48909-8150
866-685-0006
http://www.michigan.gov/dhs/0,1607,7-124-5455_27716_27718---,00.html

Minnesota

Department of Human Services
Division of Licensing
444 Lafayette Rd
St. Paul, MN 55155-3842
651-296-3971
http://www.dhs.state.mn.us/main/groups/business_partners/
documents/pub/dhs_id_028247.hcsp

Mississippi

State Dept. of Health
Division of Child Care
P.O. Box 1700
Jackson, MS 39215 - 1700
601-576-7613
http://www.msdh.state.ms.us/msdhsite/index.cfm/30,0,183,225,html

Missouri

Missouri Department of Health and Senior Services
Bureau of Child Care Safety & Licensure
1715 S. Ridge
Jefferson City, MO 65102-0570
573-751-2450
http://www.dhss.mo.gov/ChildCare/index.html

Montana

Department of Public Health and Human Services
QAD - Licensing Bureau - Child Care Licensing
P.O. Box 202953
Helena, MT 59620-2953
406-444-7770
http://www.montanachildcare.com/QAD_forms2.htm#List%20of%20Forms

Nebraska

Nebraska Health & Human Services System
Regulation and Licensure
P.O. Box 95007
301 Centennial Mall South
Lincoln, NE 68509-5007
402-471-2133 or (800) 600-1289
http://www.hhs.state.ne.us/chc/chcindex.htm

Nevada

Department of Human Resources
Division of Child and Family Services
Bureau of Services for Child Care
711 East Fifth Street
Buckland Station
Carson City, NV 89701
775-684-4463 or (800) 992-0900
http://www.leg.state.nv.us/NAC/NAC-432A.html

New Hampshire
Bureau of Child Care Licensing
129 Pleasant Street
Concord, NH 03301
800-852-3345 ext. 4624; or 603-271-4624
http://www.dhhs.state.nh.us/dhhs/bccl

New Jersey
State of New Jersey Dept. of Human Services
Office of Licensing
P.O. Box 707
Trenton, NJ 08625-0717
(800) 332-9227 or (609) 292-1018
http://www.state.nj.us/humanservices/dfd/regulatory.html

New Mexico
Children and Family Division
Child Care Services Bureau
P.O. Drawer 5160
Santa Fe, NM 87502-5160
505-827-7946 or 800-610-7610 ext. 77499
http://www.newmexicokids.org

New York
New York Department of Family Assistance
Office of Children and Family Services
Bureau of Early Childhood Services
52 Washington Street 3 N
Rensselaer, NY 12144 or
New York City Department of Health
Bureau of Day Care
2 Lafayette Street, 22nd Floor
New York, NY 10007
518-474-9454 / 212-676-2444 (for 5 boroughs)
http://www.ocfs.state.ny.us/main/becs/daycaregs.asp

North Carolina

Division of Child Development
2201 Mail Service Center
Raleigh, NC 27699-2201
919-662-4499 or 800-859-0829 (in-state only)
http://www.ncchildcare.net

North Dakota

North Dakota Department of Human Services
600 East Blvd.
Bismarck, ND 58505-0250
701-328-4809
http://www.ndchildcare.org/splash/

Ohio

Child Care Licensing Section
Department of Human Services
65 East State St. 5th Floor
Columbus, OH 43215
866-886-3537
http://jfs.ohio.gov/cdc/providers.stm#WNew

Oklahoma

Department of Human Services
Division of Child Care
P.O. Box 25352
Oklahoma City, OK 73125
405-521-3561 or (800) 347-2276
http://www.okdhs.org/childcare/

Oregon

Child Care Division
875 Union St. N.E.
Salem, OR 97311
503-947-1400 or (800) 556-6616
http://www.oregon.gov/EMPLOY/CCD/RulesSummary.shtml

Pennsylvania

Division of Regulatory Administration
Bureau of Certification Services
Office of Child Development
Department of Public Welfare
Contact Regional Office: http://www.dpw.state.pa.us/Child/
ChildCare/003670452.htm
717-787-8691 or 877-4-PA-KIDS (in-state only)
http://www.dpw.state.pa.us/Child/ChildCare/003670991.htm

Rhode Island

Rhode Island Department of Children, Youth & Families
Day Care Licensing
101 Friendship Street
Providence, RI 02903
401-528-3624
http://www.dcyf.ri.gov/day_care.php/

South Carolina

Department of Social Services
Division of Child Day Care Licensing and Regulatory Services
P.O. Box 1520, Room 520
Columbia, SC 29202-1520
803-253-4049
http://www.state.sc.us/dss/cdclrs/index.html

South Dakota

Child Care Services State of South Dakota
Richard R. Kneip Building
700 Governors Drive
Pierre, SD 57501-2291
605-773-4766 or 800-227-3020
http://www.state.sd.us/social/ccs/Licensing/regs.htm

Tennessee

Department of Human Services
Citizens Plaza
Nashville, TN 37248-9800
615-313-4778
http://www.state.tn.us/sos/rules/1240/1240-04/1240-04.htm

Texas

Texas Department of Protective & Regulatory Services
P.O. Box 149030
Mail Code E-550
Austin, TX 78714-9030
800-862-5252 or 512-438-4800
http://www.tdprs.state.tx.us/Child_Care/About_Child_Care_Licensing/
default.asp

Utah

Bureau of Licensing
Child Care Unit
288 N. 1460 West
P.O. Box 142003
Salt Lake City, UT 84114-2003
801-538-9299 or 888-287-3704
http://hlunix.hl.state.ut.us/licensing

Vermont

Child Care Services Division
103 South Main Street
Waterbury, VT 05671-2901
800-649-2642 or (802) 241-2131
http://www.state.vt.us/srs/childcare/licensing/license.htm

Virginia

Virginia Department of Social Services
Division of Licensing Programs
7 North Eighth Street
Richmond, VA 23219-3301
804-726-7143 or 800-543-7545
http://leg1.state.va.us/000/reg/TOC22015.HTM

Washington

Washington Department of Social and Health Services
Economic Services Administration
Division of Child Care and Early Learning
P.O. Box 45480
Olympia, WA 98504-5480
360-725-4665 or 866-482-4325
http://www.del.wa.gov/CCEI/policy.shtml#ccwac

West Virginia

West Virginia Department of Health and Human Resources
Office of Social Services
Division of Child Care
350 Capitol Street, Room 691
Charleston, WV 25301
Family and School 304-558-7980; Centers 304-232-4411
http://www.wvdhhr.org/bcf/ece/

Wisconsin

Bureau of Regulation and Licensing
1 West Wilson Street, Room 534
P.O. Box 8916
Madison, WI 53708-8916
608-266-9314
**http://dhfs.wisconsin.gov/rl_dcfs/INDEX.HTM or
http://www.dwd.state.wi.us/dws/programs/childcare/certification/
default.htm**

Wyoming

Department of Family Services
2300 Capitol Ave.
Hathway Building, 3rd floor
Cheyenne, WY 82002
307-777-5491
http://dfsweb.state.wy.us

Puerto Rico

Programa para el Cuidado y el Desarrolo del Niño
Pda 2 Ponce de Leon Ave
San Juan, PR 000901
787-724-7532 or 787-724-7534
msobrino@acuden.gobierno.pr

Virgin Islands

Department of Human Services
Division of Children, Youth, and Families
Knud Hansen Complex, Building A
1303 Hospital Ground
Charlotte Amalie, Virgin Islands 00802
340-774-1166

ONLINE RESOURCES

There are many places to go online to find a wealth of information regarding every aspect of childcare operations, children's health, safety policies, children's policies, staffing, and accreditation. Following are some of the best Web sites, some with a brief description of their services quoted directly from their site.

ACCREDITATION

The National Early Childhood Program Education

"The National Early Childhood Program Accreditation has been supporting educational programs striving for excellence since 1993. Our non-profit organization was created to encourage the availability of high quality early education programs for America's families. Now, as an independent and nationally recognized program, the NECPA is maintaining its pursuit for excellence by delivering its accreditation philosophy to hundreds of early childhood programs across the country."

http://www.necpa.net

Government Agencies

Council for Professional Recognition, Child Development Associate (CDA)

"The Council administers the Child Development Associate (CDA) National Credentialing Program. The CDA Program is designed to assess and credential early childhood care and education professionals based on performance."

http://www.cdacouncil.org

Child Care Online

"To champion excellence in child care by working hand in hand with parents and all members of the child care community. To focus the passion in caring for children into excellence in our undertakings."

http://childcare.net/indexnew.shtml

Crisis Management Examples

epa.gov/ogwdw/.../lead/toolkit_leadschools_3ts_telling_crisismngt.pdf

National Resource Center for Health and Safety in Child Care and Early Education.

www.nrc.uchsc.edu

National Association for Family Child Care (NAFCC)

"NAFCC is dedicated to strengthening the profession of family child care by promoting high quality, professional early care and education and strengthening communities where providers live and work."

http://www.nafcc.org/include/default.asp

National Association for the Education of Young Children (NAEYC)

"The National Association for the Education of Young Children (NAEYC) is dedicated to improving the well-being of all young children, with particular focus on the quality of educational and developmental services for all children from birth through age eight. NAEYC is committed to becoming an increasingly high performing and inclusive organization."

www.naeyc.org

National Training Institute for Child Care Health Consultants (NTI)

"A state-of-the-art national train-the-trainer program that prepares child health and child care professionals to train child care health consultants (CCHCs) in their state, territory, or community."

http://www2.sph.unc.edu/courses/childcare

National Child Care Information Center

"The National Child Care Information Center (NCCIC), a service of the Child Care Bureau, is a national clearinghouse and technical assistance center that links parents, providers, policy-makers, researchers, and the public to early care and education information."

http://nccic.org/index.html

Child and Adult Care Food Programs

"USDA's Child and Adult Care Food Program plays a vital role in improving the quality of day care and making it more affordable for many low-income families. Each day, 2.9 million children receive nutritious meals and snacks through CACFP."

http://www.fns.usda.gov/cnd/Care/CACFP/aboutcacfp.htm

Florida Department of Children and Families Gold Seal Program

"The DCF Child Care Program Office is responsible for approving accrediting agencies for participation in the Gold Seal Quality Care Program. These accrediting agencies must meet or exceed the National Association for the Education of Young Children (NAEYC) standards, the standards of the National Association of Family Child Care, or the standards of the National Early Childhood Program Accreditation Commission."

http://www.dcf.state.fl.us/childcare/goldseal.shtml

Maryland State Family Child Care Association

"The Goals and Purposes of the MSFCCA are:

- To support the local associations and associates which make up the membership of the MSFCCA.

- To represent family child care providers by educating and advising legislators, regulators, and the general public on child care issues.

- To encourage all providers to be knowledgeable of and comply with the laws governing child care in Maryland."

http://www.msfcca.org/

CONFERENCES

http://www.daycareproviders.com/confinfo.asp

STAFFING

www.employeehandbookstore.com

ART PROJECTS

Family Fun Magazine

This Web site has one of the most extensive lists for art projects. The projects cover any holiday or special occasion that a child would celebrate.

You can search for projects by materials on hand or by a theme, age, or season.

http://familyfun.go.com/arts-and-crafts/

Kaboose

The Kaboose Web site is full of great craft ideas, too. They feature searches if you want to give someone in particular a gift, such as Grandma, mom, an uncle, or a sister. They have craft categories for wearable art, art made from recycled products, and seasonal and holiday activities.

http://www.kidsdomain.com/craft/

Enchanted Learning

Enchanted Learning is a great site for child care resources. Not only do they have art and craft projects, but they offer worksheets and activities in the science and social studies fields. Their projects can be searched by date or season.

http://www.enchantedlearning.com/crafts/

DLTK's site

This site has art and craft projects for sacred and secular events. They also extend their Web site to include various games you might want to play with the children.

http://www.dltk-kids.com/

WEB GROUPS

On the Internet, there are different listservs available to child care providers.

You can join these listservs and send messages to the entire group. The listservs usually cater to specific niches, such as a hobby, profession, or activity. There are many for child care providers. Some of the lists include:

- Yahoo!

- Providers Playground

- Provider Friendship Garden

- Providers in Faith

- California Day Care Providers

The list goes on and on. Some lists require that you write to the moderator and fill out a short questionnaire before you join. Others you can subscribe to with a few clicks of the mouse. MSN, Google, and other Web hosts also provide different lists or Web rings for you to join. The lists are all free to join.

OTHER PRODUCTS OF USEFUL INFORMATION

Magazines

There are many magazines that serve the child care provider. Some include *Early Childhood News* and *Early Childhood Today*. Both are available by subscription or at bookstores. They discuss hot topics in the industry, politics about childcare and regulations, methods of improving your business, and tips for daily survival. The costs will vary between each subscription.

Newsletters

Many of the government agencies listed above offer a newsletter, either online or in print. Some may require a subscription, but many are free. A great newsletter is Totline Newsletter, full of projects and activities for preschoolers. Other newsletters are for a niche aspect in your business. For example, the group who monitors your food program may send out a monthly newsletter full of recipes, suggestions for menu planning, and articles on the current state of the policy. The newsletter has a focused point and is in direct relation to a portion of your business.

Outsourcing Resources

When you just do not know how or lack the time to write, you can outsource your work. There are many sites that act as liaisons for not only freelance writers, but also designers, marketers, and office professionals. Some of the top sites are listed below:

- **www.elance.com**
- **www.guru.com**
- **www.ifreelance.com**
- **www.sologig.com**
- **www.writerlance.com**

You can post your project or what you need done, and the freelancers who are available and willing to do that project will bid. With sites that use a bidding process, you will also get a fair price since they are competing against one another.

"Tell me and I'll forget; show me and I may remember;

involve me and I'll understand."

~ Chinese Proverbs

APPENDIX B

SAMPLES

The following are samples that are ready for use by your business. Some you can simply copy; others you can adapt to fit your exact needs.

Press Release

A press release follows a simple format. You can place it on your letterhead or use a blank sheet of paper. Fill in your contact information at the top. Use a two word summary at the top, followed by one or two paragraphs describing your story. Press releases should be short and to the point, but should interest the readers so they feel your story is newsworthy and will pick it up. A press release needs to be presented as a professional document to other professionals. When it is sloppy, poorly written, or it does not follow a format, it will be disregarded. Take the time to learn how to do it properly or hire someone to do it.

SAMPLE PRESS RELEASE

News Release

Teddy Bear Preschool
12345 My Street
My Town, State, US

Contact: Child Care Owner (name)
Phone: 999-555-1212
Fax: 999-555-1212
E-mail: teddybearpreschool@

For Immediate Release

Teddy Bear Preschool in Mytown Celebrates Earth Day
Children learn the importance of protecting the environment

Freeland, Michigan, April 20, 2007: The Teddy Bear Preschool celebrated Earth Day by planting trees at the local park. One hundred white pine trees were donated by the Garden Club and planted in designated locations around the 100 acre park. The head of the nature center was on hand to teach children the importance of trees in keeping our air clean.

The Teddy Bear Preschool incorporates how children can take care of the Earth in its daily curriculum message. The preschool is accredited and meets stringent guidelines for curriculum in science and developmental topics. Visit the Teddy Bear Preschool online at **www.teddybearpreschool.com** for more information and to see pictures of recent activities.

###

Newspaper Ad

This is only one style of ad you can place in the classifieds section of a newspaper. If you are advertising in a section with graphics and logos, have the newspaper design one for you. Often times they will do it for a small fee or you can hire someone to do it for you.

SAMPLE NEWSPAPER AD
Teddy Bear Preschool in (city) has openings for the 2007-2008 school year. Accredited program, great rates, convenient hours and location. Open house 8/25/07 from 6 p.m. until 8 p.m. Free cookies. Call (999) 555-1212 for more information and directions.

Bio

You should have a bio prepared and put in your media kit. This way, you can give it to prospective clients at a moment's notice. They will quickly begin to see your credentials in the child care industry.

SAMPLE BIO
My name is Tina Musial and I have recently opened a child care center in my home. I am licensed to care for children in my home between the hours of 7 a.m. and 5:30 p.m.
My background includes child development classes through the state agency. I have attended:
Behavior management
Developmental milestones for infants
Developmental milestones for toddlers
Cooking for Picky Eaters
I am Red Cross CPR and first aid training certified. I have worked in large child care centers for five years prior to opening my own center.
Teddy Bear Preschool A – 1997-1999

SAMPLE BIO

Teddy Bear Preschool C – 2003 - 2006

I will provide a loving, fun, and safe environment for your child to grow.

I belong to the following organizations:

NAEYC
NFCC
NCICC

READY TO USE FORMS

SAMPLE HOURS OF OPERATION

Hours of Operation

Monday through Friday

7 a.m. until 5:30 pm

Late fees

$5 for every 15 minute interval starting at 5:25 p.m.

For every third instance, there will be an additional charge of $10.

SAMPLE INTERVIEW SHEET

Name: _____

Date: _____

Interest Level: _____

Parent Demeanor: _____

Children Present?: Yes: _____ No: _____

Children's Demeanor: _____

Tour Given?: Yes: _____ No: _____

Questions Asked: _____

_____

_____

_____

Notes: _____

_____

_____

_____

Staff Signature: _____

SAMPLE ENROLLMENT FORM

Name of Child: _____

Age: _____

Date of Birth: _____

Special Needs: _____

Allergies: _____

_____

Care is needed: Full Time: _____ Part Time: _____

Days/Hours:

Monday: _____

Tuesday: _____

Wednesday: _____

Thursday: _____

Friday: _____

Saturday: _____

Sunday: _____

Parent Name: _____

Address: _____

_____

Staff Use Only

Date Enrolled: _____

Date Left:_____

SAMPLE CONTRACT

This agreement is made between _____
_____ (daycare provider) and _____
_____ (child care recipient) on _____
_____ (date).

Care for _____ (children's
names) will begin on _____ (date)
_____ (time).

Hours of care needed will be approximately _____
_____ (time) to _____ (time) on the following
days: _____
_____.

Cost for care will be $ _____ per week, payable on __
_____ (day). If the fee is not paid, there will be a late fee of $
_____ added on for each day the payment is late.

In the event that care is no longer needed, the child care recipient will give the child care provider two weeks' notice. If two weeks' notice is not given, the child care provider shall still receive two weeks worth of compensation at the agreed rate.

SAMPLE MEDICAL FORM

Child's Name: _____

Physician's Name: _____

Current Health: _____

_____

Concerns: _____

_____

_____

_____

Immunizations Current: _____

_____

_____

_____

PhysicalDisabilities/Limitations:_____

_____

_____

_____

SAMPLE VACATION SCHEDULE

During the year 2007, I will be closed the following dates:

January 1st

April 8th

May 27th

June 11-14

July 4th

August 28th

September 3rd

November 27-28

December 24-25

Please make alternate arrangements for care on these days. If you have any questions, feel free to call me and we can discuss it.

SAMPLE INCIDENT REPORT

Name of Child: _____

Name of reporting staff member: _____

Additional staff present: _____

_____

_____

Date: _____

Description of Incident: _____

_____

_____

_____

Resolution _____

_____

_____

_____

Signature of reporting staff: _____

_____

SAMPLE INJURY REPORT

Name of Child: _____

Name of reporting staff member: _____

Additional staff present: _____

_____

_____

Date: _____

Time of Injury: _____

Parents Called? Yes: _____ No: _____ Time: _____

Description of injury: _____

_____

_____

_____

Care Given: _____

_____

_____

_____

Signature of reporting staff: _____

SAMPLE CONFIDENTIALITY OF RECORDS

Your child's records, medical history, and information will never be shared with outside parties or displayed online. Your child's privacy is of the utmost concern to us. The records are kept in a locked file cabinet and only used for meeting licensing regulations.

SAMPLE INFANT SCHEDULE

Date: _____

Name: _____

We had a Great _____ OK _____ not so great _____
day.

Today, I had a bottle at: _____
_____ (times)

I had a bowel movement at: _____
_____

I took naps at: _____
_____

SAMPLE PICTURE PERMISSION

I give my permission to _____
_____ (name of provider) to take photographs of
my child _____
(name of child). I understand these pictures may be shared in marketing
and publicity materials. My child's name will not be shared nor will any
of their personal information be released.

Signature: _____

Date: _____

SAMPLE SUNSCREEN PERMISSION

I give my permission to _____
_____ (name of provider) to apply sunscreen
on my child _____
(name of child) anytime they go outdoors, and it is deemed necessary.

Signature:_____

Date: _____

SAMPLE INSECT REPELLANT PERMISSION

I give my permission to _____
_____ (name of provider) to apply insect repellant to my
child _____
(name of child) anytime it is deemed necessary outdoors.

Signature:_____

Date: _____

SAMPLE FIELD TRIP PERMISSION

I give my permission to _____
_____ (child care provider) to transport my child _____
_____
(name) to _____
(location of field trip) on _____ (date).

Signature _____

SAMPLE EMPLOYEE INTERVIEW QUESTIONS

Prospective name_____

Date _____

Do you have any experience working with children?

   What ages?

   Where?

   How long?

Where else do you interact with children?

What is your discipline policy?

What do you like best about working with children?

What is your least favorite part of child care?

Can you work the hours of (hours you need)?

Can you perform the tasks specified in the job description? (provide list of job duties)

Do you have any questions for me?

SAMPLE JOB DESCRIPTION FORM

Job description for assistant caregiver in _____ (age group)

- Manage children in the said age group appropriately

- Administer medicine to children as needed

- Serve morning snack and lunch to children

- Clean using the three step sanitation method

- Alternate cleaning the children's bathroom with other staff members

- Supervise indoor and outdoor playtime

- Assist in creating and leading craft projects

- Inform parents of daily activities of the children

- Attend monthly training sessions

- Assist children in tidying up the room at the end of the day

- Assist in nap time preparation

This job may require you to be able to lift 50 pounds and work outside during playtime.

SAMPLE EMPLOYEE DISCIPLINE FORM

This is to signify you have received a verbal warning for actions pertaining to _____ (date). This is your _____ (number warning) and you are allowed _____ (number) before you will be terminated.

SAMPLE EMPLOYEE REVIEW FORM

Employee Name_____

Date Reviewed_____

Reviewed By_____

With one being the lowest and five being the highest, rate the employee in the following categories:

Punctual? 1_____ 2_____ 3_____ 4_____ 5_____

Continuously care for children in an efficient and positive manner?

1_____ 2_____ 3 _____ 4 _____ 5 _____

Treat other employees and parents with respect?

1 _____ 2_____ 3 _____ 4_____ 5 _____

Complete all assigned tasks and job duties?

1 _____ 2 _____ 3 _____ 4 _____ 5 _____

Current on training? Yes _____ No _____

Raise given? Yes_____ No _____ Amount_____

Notes:

_____

_____

_____

_____

PARENT EVALUATION

A parent evaluation can be handed out yearly to everyone in your services or you can create a packet for each family based on the anniversary of their start date. If you give the surveys out to everyone at the same time, you are assured everyone gets one. You may be overwhelmed by the volume of paperwork for a few days, however. If you opt to give them at intervals spread over the year, it may become confusing and you may also forget to give them out, resulting in lost evaluations.

SAMPLE PARENT EVALUATION FORM

This is an annual evaluation of our services. Please respond honestly with where you enjoy our services or where you believe they can be improved. You can remain anonymous with your evaluation or you can place your name at the top. If you would like to be contacted to personally speak about your evaluation, please call me or stop in my office anytime to set up an appointment.

Please rate your satisfaction with the following services, with one being very dissatisfied and five being very satisfied.

Our hours are convenient?   ___1 ___2 ___ 3 ___4 ___5

Are staff friendly and informative?   ___1 ___2 ___3 ___4 ___5

You are satisfied with the food served ___ 1 ___2 ___3 ___4 ___5

The rates are fair and reasonable   ___ 1 ___2 ___3 ___4 ___5

The area (my house) is clean and safe ___ 1 ___ 2 ___ 3 ___ 4 ___ 5

My child likes to come to the center   ___1 ___2 ___3 ___4 ___5

What optional services do you currently use? _____

_____

_____

_____

SAMPLE PARENT EVALUATION FORM

How satisfied are you with those services? _____

_____

_____

What do you like best about my child care center? _____

_____

_____

Are there any areas of concern you have? _____

_____

_____

Do you have any comments? _____

_____

_____

Name (optional) _____

Do you wish to be contacted? _____

Thank you for taking the time to fill out this survey. Each family that completes a survey and uses their name will be entered in to a drawing for a gift certificate to McDonald's.

GLOSSARY

Abuse: Harmful verbal, emotional, or sexual infliction upon another person.

Accreditation: Specific standards that child care centers must meet in order to receive an endorsement from a professional agency.

Advocacy: A group of people (parents, volunteers, organizations, etc.) who work together to protect the rights of others.

Affordability: The rates for child care expense will vary from city to city. It is pertinent that the cost of child care a realistic family expense. This can be determined by what other child care facilities in the area charge, as well as by the cost of living in a particular area.

Age Groupings: Infant – a newborn to 9 months

Toddler – 9 to 18 months

Older Toddler: 18 to 24 months

Preschool: 24 to 48 months

School Aged: 48 months and older

Anti-social Behavior: When a child acts the opposite of the socially acceptable behavior

Assessment: Written observations on a child's performance. Areas that may be included in an assessment vary but can include: motor skills, self-help skills, language skills, social skills, emotional skills, cognitive skills, and intellectual skills.

Emotional Attachment: The psychological bond that a child has with another person.

Attachment Disorder: A child's inability to develop emotional connections with other people.

Attention Deficit Disorder: The inability for a child to sustain attention to an activity and control his or her behavior.

Attention Deficit Hyperactivity Disorder: Similar to ADD, this includes excessive over-activity, such as restlessness, running, and talking.

Auditory Discrimination: Where a child may have difficulty distinguishing the difference between various speech sounds and being able to identify those particular sounds correctly.

Behavior Modification: A way to change a particular, usually unacceptable, behavior.

Behavioral Disorders: Atypical behaviors that can be influenced by biological or environmental means. These disorders can include such symptoms as self-injuring behavior, strong aggression, hyperactivity, withdrawal, etc.

Benefits: As an owner of a business, you must decide what benefits to offer employees. In a child care center, these benefits can range from health insurance to child care for their children to free meals.

Bilingual: Where a person has the ability to speak and comprehend two languages fluently.

Block Grant: Money supplied by the federal government to state and local governments in an effort to support social welfare programs.

Capacity: The total number of children that can be enrolled at a child care center. This will vary based on the size of the center and the size of the center's staff.

Caregiver: One who provides children with protection and care in or outside of the home.

Certification: Credentials awarded to an individual that state that he or she satisfactorily completed and demonstrated a particular knowledge or skill.

Child Care Center: A business that provides care for children for short periods of time.

Child Development: The ways in which children develop skills through the use of speech and physical activity. The skills can be acquired through social, emotional, and intellectual endeavors.

Child Passenger Restraint Device: A protection, such as a car seat, seat belt, or booster seat, that is used to protect a child while he or she is traveling in a car.

Child Protective Services: An agency that is responsible for investigating any report of suspected child neglect or abuse.

Children's Health Insurance Program: A program by the U.S. federal government that allows states to give health insurance care to uninsured children.

Cognitive Delays: A delay in a child's thinking and reasoning skills.

Comprehension: The ability of a child to understanding the meaning of a particular subject matter.

Comprehensive Services: Services that promote a child's development that are offered to families.

Concept Development: A child's comprehension of specific ideas or thoughts that relate to different topics, such as size, shapes, etc.

Consumer Education: Information that is provided to caregivers in an effort to educate them on quality child care.

Corporation: When a business is owned by a group of people who are all shareholders in the business. These shareholders own stock in the company and help direct the way the company is run.

Cost-of-Living Adjustment: Any changes to wages or service fees as a result of inflation.

CPR: Cardio Pulmonary Resuscitation covers all breathing emergencies. This training provides instructions on handling choking, heart stoppages, and blocked airways.

Creativity: The way a child expresses his or herself demonstrating the use of imagination and originality.

Cultural Awareness: Respecting and understanding the customs and values of people that come from different backgrounds.

Curriculum: Designed areas of instruction that help teach children a specific skill or give them knowledge in a specific area.

Custodial Parent: The primary care giver of a minor child.

Developmental Appropriate Practice: Support of a child's learning process through the means of a suitable curriculum.

Developmental Disabilities: Conditions or disorders that may hinder a child's cognitive abilities.

Developmental Milestones: Memorable achievements in a child's growth, such as rolling over, talking, walking, etc.

Developmental Stages: The sequential order that a child develops certain behaviors. An example would be that a child would normally learn to crawl before he or she can walk.

Drop Off Child Care Centers: Centers that provide temporary child care while parents are able to run errands or attend to other business.

Drop In Care: A center that may allow unscheduled or back up care as necessary.

Dyslexia: A condition where the brain cannot process information correctly. This condition results in a difficulty for a child to read, spell, or write.

Employer Income Tax Credits: These tax credits are available to child care business who provide income assistance for families by means of paying for part of their child care expenses.

Employer Child Care: A child care setting that may offer benefits to the employees of a company because the center may be on-site or near the place of employment.

Extended Day Program: A program for school-aged children that offers care and teaching after school hours.

Family Assessment: Information gathered on a family that helps observe the family's strengths and weaknesses, and addresses any concerns that the family may have in regard to their child's development.

Family Assistance: Programs, either state or federal, that provide families with monetary assistance in means of income, health care, child care, housing, etc.

Family Support Services: Programs in the community that help families develop parenting skills.

Financial Assistance: Monetary assistance from businesses or community organizations that help off-set child care costs.

Food Program: Usually a voluntary program that a child care center can belong to that provides for part of the cost of food. A child care center must serve food based on a certain criteria. States will do random inspections of the child care center to make sure that it is meeting the criteria.

Franchise: A license granted by a company to individuals to use its name to market its products or services in a specific location.

Free Play: A time which children can choose their own activity.

Gross Motor Control: The ability to use large muscles for balancing and movement to better engage in activities, such as walking, running, or sports.

Guardian: A person who has legal authority to care for child.

Hand-Eye Coordination: The ability to use the hand and eye to work together in order to achieve the completion of a task.

Ill Child Care: Child care services that are provided to mildly sick children.

Income Eligible: A family that meets the state requirements to have a subsidy for child care.

Individualized Education Plan: A curriculum developed especially for a child that has special needs. It will help the child become more adept at certain tasks or areas of learning.

Infant Stimulation Programs: Special programs that help enhance the sensory and cognitive development of infants.

Inspections: A state representative will inspect your child care business location much like an appraiser of your home would. These inspections are random and are required to make sure that your child care business meets specific criteria.

Insurance: There are many different types of insurance. Though insurance may not be required by a specific state, it is good to have in case of an accident.

> **Structural Insurance:** Protects against damage to your business

> **Liability Insurance:** Protects against any accidents that occur on your property

> **Health Insurance:** Supplements health care costs

> **Worker's Compensation:** Supplements income in the event of an accident

Learning Disability: A difficulty that a child has in a particular skill area. This learning disability is not related to intelligence or educational opportunity.

Learning Styles: The different ways that a child adapts to a learning environment.

Licensed Child Care: Child care programs approved by the state that meet specific regulations.

Licensing: Varies by state. Every child care center is required to have a license to be in operation.

Mainstreaming: Immersing children with disabilities into non-special education classes for part or all of the school day.

Manipulative Toy: Toys that help children develop fine-motor skills and hand-eye coordination.

Medicaid: A program that allows for medical care for low-income families or persons with developmental disabilities. This program is funded by the U.S. federal government.

Mental Health: How a person reacts to life's situations in regards to making decisions, handling other people, and dealing with stress.

Mixed-Age Grouping: Combining various aged children in one setting.

Motor Skills: The ability to use large and small muscle groups.

Non-Custoidal Parent: In a divorced family, this is the parent that does not have custody over the child.

Non-Traditional Child Care: This type of care can also be known as "after hours care." It is care that is provided for children before or after work hours and on the weekend.

Parent: The person(s) responsible for the child. The person can be either biological, adoptive, or a legal guardian.

Partnership: When more than one person goes into business. A partnership requires an agreement or a written contract which details each person's involvement in the business.

Physical Disabilities: Specific disorders that reduce bodily functions.

Print Awareness: The ability of a child to understand the rules of the written language, and the ability to understand letters, numbers, and spaces.

Professional Development: A child care worker's ongoing training to increase their ability to handle and provide care for children.

Quality Assurance: A specific set of activities that ensure the safety of the children receiving the child care services.

Read Aloud: An activity that engages children in reading, either by having someone read aloud to them or by having the children read aloud in a group.

Receptive Language Skills: The ability of a child to comprehend others' spoken or written words.

Referral: A person who received knowledge of your child care center by the means of someone else.

School Readiness: A state in a child's early development life that will further enable them to benefit from learning experiences.

Screening: Assessing a child and his or her family to see if they meet the criteria for your child care center.

Sensory-Motor Skills: A child's exploration of the five senses.

Separation Anxiety: A child's uneasiness in relation to the separation from his or her parent.

Sliding Fee Scale: This scale allows for the adjustment of child care fees based on income.

Socialization: How a child becomes familiar with society.

Sole Proprietorship: When only one person owns the business.

Special Needs Child: A child under the age of 18 that requires special attention in some facet of life.

Staff: State restrictions are specific as to how many children a person can care for. A background check is also required for all staff members.

Title 1: A program that provides additional support for children that need instruction or assistance. This is only for eighth grade and below.

Transition: A change from one environment to another.

Unlicensed Child Care: A child care facility that has not applied or met the state's requirements for operation.

Unregulated Child Care: Programs that are not monitored by a state regulating agency.

BIBLIOGRAPHY

Copeland, Tom JD. *Contracts & Policies: How to be Businesslike in a Caring Profession.* Redleaf Press, St. Paul, Minnesota. Second Edition, 1997.

Copeland, Tom JD. *Marketing Guide: How to Build Enrollment and promote Your Business As a Child Care Professional,* Redleaf Press, St. Paul Minnesota, 1999.

Gallagher, Patricia C. *So You Want To Open A Profitable Child Care Center: Everything You Need to Know to Plan, Organize & Implement a Successful Program.* Mosby, Inc. St. Louis, Missouri, 1995.

Jack, Gail. *The Business of Child Care: Management and Financial Strategies.* Thomson Delmar Learning, United States, 2005.

Lynn, Jacquelyn and Entrepreneur Press. *Start Your Own Child Care Service: Your Step By Step Guide to Success.* Entrepreneur Press, 2006.

Sciarra, Dorothy June and Anne G. Dorsey. *Opening & Operating: A Successful Child Care Center.* Delmar Thomson learning, 2002.

AUTHOR BIOGRAPHY

Tina Musial

Tina Musial "grew up" in a home-based child care center. After years of having other children move in and out of the family while they were being cared for, she saw how the intricacies of the business worked. Home child care appeared to be a challenging, but very rewarding business.

After college, Tina worked in several small and large child care centers, both independent and within a franchise. Even though a child care center is a child care center, wherever it is based, there are many differences between home and the center. And now having her own children in child care centers, she has come full circle and been on all sides of the situation. She can be contacted at **tmmsmail@yahoo.com**.

INDEX

THE COMPLETE GUIDE TO UNDERSTANDING, CONTROLLING, AND STOPPING BULLIES & BULLYING: A COMPLETE GUIDE

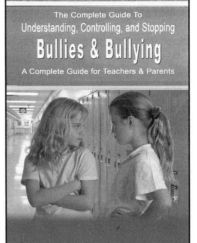

The Complete Guide To
Understanding, Controlling, and Stopping
Bullies & Bullying
A Complete Guide for Teachers & Parents

In April 2007, 32 students were killed during the Virginia Polytechnic Institute and State University shooting. According to MSNBC news services, the student gunman was bullied and mocked by his classmates.

Given that most bullying goes unnoticed and unreported, Americans have been slow to react to behavior that is taking over our schools. Other countries deal with mean people, while in the United States, take-charge insolence, no matter how threatening, is rewarded in schools, in business, in sports, and in everyday life. Often those who stand up to a bully suffer retribution so that their only defense seems to be to turn to violence themselves.

This book will teach you will know how to evaluate the bullying problem in your school, develop anger management and conflict resolution skills, develop awareness of the problem, learn victim role playing and assertiveness training, and many other important skills on handling bullies and bullying in your school.

All children deserve the right to go to school free of intimidation. Help make your school bully-free.

ISBN-10: 1-60138-021-6 • ISBN-13: 978-1-60138-021-0
288 Pages • $24.95

To order call 1-800-814-1132 or visit www.atlantic-pub.com

EMPLOYEE BODY LANGUAGE REVEALED: HOW TO PREDICT BEHAVIOR IN THE WORKPLACE BY READING AND UNDERSTANDING BODY LANGUAGE

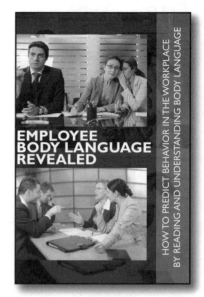

Only 7 percent of communication is verbal and 38 percent is vocal. The largest chunk then, 55 percent, is visual. People form 90 percent of their opinion about you within the first 90 seconds of meeting you. Understanding body language is a skill that can enhance your life. This understanding can be a plus in the workplace. You can know what an employee or co-worker thinks and feels by examining their subconscious body language. And, like the world's best communicators, you can have strong body language that reflects confidence, competence, and charisma.

This groundbreaking new book will make you an expert on body language. You will have the ability to read people's minds. Would you like to know if a co-worker is interested or attracted to you, when an employee or co-worker is lying or telling the truth, how to make instant friends, and persuade and influence others? This book contains proven techniques that will make people, including employers and co-workers, like you and trust you. You can use your body language to your advantage by transmitting only the messages you want people to receive. This specialized book will demonstrate step by step how to use body language to your benefit in the workplace and in everyday situations.

ISBN-10: 1-60138-147-6 • ISBN-13: 978-1-60138-147-7
288 Pages • $21.95

To order call 1-800-814-1132 or visit www.atlantic-pub.com

101 Businesses You Can Start With Less Than One Thousand Dollars: For Stay-at-Home Moms & Dads

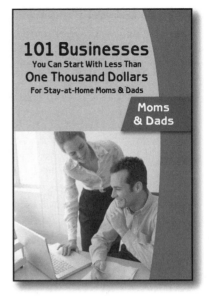

Many parents today have a tough time economically; they need two incomes, yet would like to be home with their children. A small business can be the perfect solution! This is a collection of over 100 businesss selected espeically for stay-at-home parents. All can be operated from home.

Starting and managing a business takes motivation and talent. It also takes research and planning. This new book is intended to serve as a road map for starting your business. It is both comprehensive and easy to use. It also includes numerous web links for additional information. While providing detailed instruction and examples, the author leads you in developing a winning business plan, structuring the business, handling legal concerns, using proven sales and marketing techniques and pricing formulas, learning how to set up computer systems to save time and money, generating high-profile public relations and publicity, learning low-cost internal marketing ideas and low- and no-cost ways to satisfy customers and build sales, learning how to keep bringing customers back, accounting and bookkeeping procedures, as well as thousands of great tips and useful guidelines.

ISBN-10: 0-910627-88-6 • ISBN-13: 978-910627-88-7
288 Pages • $21.95

THE COMPLETE GUIDE TO UNDERSTANDING, CONTROLLING, & STOPPING BULLIES & BULLYING AT WORK:
A COMPLETE GUIDE FOR MANAGERS, SUPERVISORS, AND CO-WORKERS

According to the Occupational Safety and Health Administration (OSHA), more than two million workers in the United States alone are victims of workplace violence each year, leading to millions of dollars lost in employee productivity. Many people believe that bullying occurs only among school-age children and fail to acknowledge the presence and devastation effects of bullying in the workplace.

In this new book, you will learn how to identify the problem of workplace bullying, how to define the workplace bully, how to identify characteristics of workplace bullies, how to bust bullying, and how to "bully-proof" your employees. This book discusses indicators of a toxic workplace, the causes of workplace bullying, and reasons why workplace bullying is perpetuated and unchallenged by other employees.

This book also provides solutions to end workplace violence. If you are a manager, a supervisor, or an employee and you suspect bullying is occurring, you need to read this book.

ISBN-10: 1-60138-236-7 • ISBN-13: 978-1-60138-236-8
288 Pages • $21.95

GETTING CLIENTS AND KEEPING CLIENTS FOR YOUR BUSINESS: A 30-DAY STEP-BY-STEP PLAN FOR BUILDING YOUR BUSINESS

Many books are written on how to attract more business for retail stores or new products, but this is the only book written for the small business service provider. Whether you are an attorney, doctor, accountant, consultant, personal trainer, insurance agent, Web or computer consultant, graphic designer, dentist, landscape or pool caretaker, professional cleaner, wedding planner, tree trimmer, caterer, or pet sitter, this book is for you.

The truth is unless you keep a steady stream of clients coming through your doors, you will never be as successful as you would really like to be. If you're great at working with clients and you do an excellent job of providing your services, you have the capability to turn your service business into a highly profitable firm, easily.

This specialized book will demonstrate methodically how to market and promote your services—easily, inexpensively, and most important—profitably. You will learn how to find new business clients quickly and keep existing ones satisfied by selling client based solutions and services by putting technology and low-cost marketing devices into place that take little or no time on your part.

ISBN-10: 1-60138-044-5 • ISBN-13: 978-1-60138-044-9
288 Pages • $24.95

DID YOU BORROW THIS COPY?

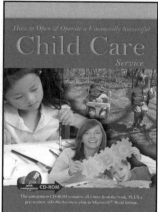

Have you been borrowing a copy of *How to Open & Operate a Financially Successful Child Care Service: With Companion CD-ROM* from a friend, colleague, or library? Wouldn't you like your own copy for quick and easy reference? To order, photocopy the form below and send to:

Atlantic Publishing Company
1405 SW 6th Ave • Ocala, FL 34471-0640

Order toll-free 800-814-1132
FAX 352-622-1875

Atlantic Publishing Company
1405 SW 6th Ave • Ocala, FL 34471-0640

Add $7.00 for USPS shipping and handling. For Florida residents PLEASE add the appropriate sales tax for your county.